ANIMALIA

An Anti-Imperial Bestiary
for Our Times

ANIMALIA

An Anti-Imperial Bestiary

for Our Times

Edited by

Antoinette Burton *&* Renisa Mawani

DUKE UNIVERSITY PRESS · DURHAM AND LONDON · 2020

© 2020 DUKE UNIVERSITY PRESS
Printed in the United States of America on acid-free paper ∞
Designed by Matthew Tauch
Typeset in SangBleu by Copperline Book Services

Library of Congress Cataloging-in-Publication Data
Names: Burton, Antoinette M., [dates]. | Mawani, Renisa, [dates].
Title: Animalia : an anti-imperial bestiary for our times / edited by
Antoinette Burton and Renisa Mawani.
Description: Durham : Duke University Press, 2020. | Includes index.
Identifiers: LCCN 2020014218 (print) | LCCN 2020014219 (ebook) |
ISBN 9781478010234 (hardcover) | ISBN 9781478011286 (paperback) |
ISBN 9781478012818 (ebook)
Subjects: LCSH: Animal culture—England—History—19th century. | Animals—England—
History—19th century. | Animals—Social aspects—England—History—19th century. |
Human-animal relationships—England—History—19th century. | Animal welfare—
England—History—19th century. | Animal culture—England—History—20th century. |
Animals—England—History—20th century. | Animals—Social aspects—England—
History—20th century. | Human-animal relationships—England—History—20th
century. | Animal welfare—England—History—20th century. | Great Britain—
Colonies—Social life and customs.
Classification: LCC SF53 .A556 2020 (print) | LCC SF53 (ebook) | DDC 636.00942—dc23
LC record available at https://lccn.loc.gov/2020014218
LC ebook record available at https://lccn.loc.gov/2020014219

Cover art: Details of illustrations from George Shaw, *Zoological Lectures
Delivered at the Royal Institution in the Years 1806 and 1807* (1809).

CONTENTS

ACKNOWLEDGMENTS

This project has been several years in the making, and we have accrued a number of debts we'd like to acknowledge here. Our first is to Miriam Angress, our editor at Duke, who has been a champion of the concept from the start. She has been tireless in keeping it going in the face of what felt like a combination of both big hurdles and minutiae; we are truly grateful. Our second is to the contributors, who also held fast through many rounds of revision. We owe a special thanks to Utathya Chattopadhyaya, who saved us at the last minute without, apparently, even breaking a sweat.

I (Antoinette) would like to thank Gus Wood and Beth Ann Williams, whose research assistance has been invaluable for generating an ongoing "animalia" archive. Tom Bedwell of the Department of History at the University of Illinois makes so many things possible; I am truly forever in his debt. I'd like to acknowledge the support of the Swanlund family, without whom my research efforts would be much the poorer. Nancy Castro is a daily lifeline, for which I thank her. Paul is second to none. And in addition to being an intellectual partner and indispensable interlocutor, Renisa Mawani has become the dearest friend one could wish for, thanks in large part to the years we have spent (mainly on email!) working on this book. I am so happy we are in the same universe.

I (Renisa) would like to thank Stefano Pantaleone for his research assistance and his overall enthusiasm for this project; the University of British Columbia for various sources of funding, including the Hampton Research Grant for "Insect Jurisprudence" that allowed me to think seriously with animal worlds; and Riaz, for reminding me of all that fills the universe, and for being mine. Most of all, my deepest gratitude goes to Antoinette Burton for inviting me to conceptualize and complete *Animalia* with her. This has been a collaboration in the best possible sense. It has fulfilled my hopes and expectations of what an intellectual partnership should and can be. Through this bestiary, we have nurtured each other's creativity and developed a deep friendship, for which I am deeply grateful and from which I continue to learn so much.

Together, we'd like to dedicate this book to our children, Lialah, Nick, Olivia, and Sayeed, for their imagination, inspiration, and, most of all, for teaching us how to live in more-than-human worlds.

INTRODUCTION

Animals, Disruptive Imperial Histories, and the Bestiary Form

How trivial these symbols look; the simplest things we show to childhood!
But a sleeping force lies within them that revolutionizes the world.

LUTHER MARSH, ADDRESS ON THE ALPHABET,

THE VEHICLE OF HISTORY (1885)

The British Empire was entangled in animal life at every possible scale. Whether as imaginative resources, military vehicles, settler foodstuffs, status emblems, contested signs, or motors of capital, animals drove both the symbolic and political economy of modern imperialism wherever it took root. If imperial sovereignty was biopolitical—determining who could live and who must die—it was because the quest for racial supremacy was a pursuit of species supremacy and vice versa. And if empire was a project dedicated to organizing hierarchies of lives worth living, the human/animal distinction served as a recurrent reference point for who was expendable and who would flourish. How we talk about the animalia of empire, then, is critical to how we narrate the force of imperial power, including its unruly targets and its disruptive histories.

By foregrounding the British Empire as a multispecies enterprise, this bestiary offers one format and orientation for thinking through the workings of imperial power. Focused on a wide range of nonhuman animals—domestic, feral, mythical, and predatory—the collection invites readers to take stock of "animalia," the taxonomic "kingdom" category first developed by Carl Linnaeus in his *Systema Naturæ* (1735), which informed and shaped nineteenth- and twentieth-century British imperial thought. By exploring human/animal relations of various kinds, the volume offers a critical reflection on how racial assertions of species supremacy played out in animal form. It tracks the ways Victorian "animal dreams" were bound up in imperial aspirations and vice versa. Representations of species supremacy were and are visual aids not simply to mark the unstable boundary between the human and nonhuman animal, but to highlight the history of dissent and disruption they index.[1] As an A to Z of animals and empire, *Animalia* illustrates how, why, and under what conditions the Anglophone imperial world was shaped and troubled by a variety of creatures—real, imagined, and underfoot.

To be clear, the bestiary was not an especially popular modern European genre; nor was it a common imperial one. Its heyday was in the middle ages, where it was an aesthetic object with a pedagogical purpose, most often as an instrument of catechism. A category of "illustrated ABC" texts emerged in English from the eighteenth century onward. Some of these dealt with animals, especially in the Victorian period, where X IS FOR *XERUS* and Y IS FOR YAK might appear complete with semiscientific images in children's books. But these abecedarium texts were not dedicated exclusively to animals, imperial or otherwise. Anglophone readers had access to a vast array of animal portraits and images—from the paintings of Stubbs and Landseer to zoological drawings both scientific and popular—that suffused modern British culture. The visual field had primacy in this domain.[2] Given the centrality of animals to the English imagination, and their indispensability to the workings of the modern British Empire, the lack of a text-based bestiary form seems counterintuitive. If the bestiary is broadly defined as a classification tool—a naming device—designed to order and arrange the living world through a combination of words and images, then a wide range of nineteenth-century texts including natural histories, children's fictional books, *Boys' Own* stories, and even "memoirs" like Richard Owen's on the gorilla, might be said to be bestiaries by another name.[3] Format is key. As Luther Marsh notes in the opening epigraph above, classification systems—in his case, the English alphabet—may at first seem trivial, but "a sleeping force lies within them," one that organizes, taxonomizes, and potentially "revolutionizes the world." We follow Marsh's provocation and use the English alphabet as one possible format for considering how the British Empire organized scientific and popular knowledge on humans and animals in the Anglo imperial world. We also use it to index the ways these taxonomic orders were disputed and disrupted by animals and humans alike.

Charles Knight's two-volume *Pictorial Museum of Animated Nature*, published in 1844, offers one example of popular animal knowledge in the Victorian period. A comprehensive survey of mammals (elephants, jackals, oxen, and bats) and birds (warblers, wrens, and honey-sucklers), Knight's catalogue is arguably a bestiary, albeit not in alphabetized form. The same might be said of John Lockwood Kipling's lavishly illustrated *Man and Beast in India*. First published in 1891, the book begins with an epigraph from Walt Whitman:

> *I think I could turn and live with animals, they are so placid*
> *   and self-contained*
> *I stand and look at them long and long.*
> *They do not sweat and whine about their condition,*
> *They do not lie in the dark and weep for their sins,*
> *They do not make me sick discussing their duty to God,*
> *Not one is dissatisfied, not one is demented with the mania*
> *   of owning things.*

Idealized via a critique of God and Mammon in Whitman's poem, animals in Kipling's text serve a distinctly racial and imperial purpose. They support his argument that, contrary to popular opinion, Queen Victoria's colonial subjects were as cruel, if not more so, than Britons in their treatment of animals. Written at a moment when the cow-protection movement in India was gaining prominence, and in the wake of the passage of an animal rights act, *Man and Beast in India* is an attack on what British authorities viewed to be Hindu and Muslim practices of animal brutality. The well-being of animals was a primer for why the British should continue ruling India and remain vigilant in their civilizing mission, for the sake of the creaturely world, if nothing else.[4]

If bestiaries, strictly speaking, were not a common imperial form, books that elaborated taxonomies of animal life were. Volumes and periodicals abounded in and across the British Empire, from expansion through decolonization and beyond. The discipline of zoology took off at the high mark of Victorian empire. Textbooks on the subject, whether written from the perspective of the field or the laboratory, offered history lessons for medical students and students of empire alike. The writings of Charles Darwin, including his 1871 *Descent of Man*, and those of his contemporaries, such as George Romanes's 1882 *Animal*

Intelligence, are a small part of the vast nineteenth-century archive of animalia that made its way into the hands of professional and lay readers. These writings spawned new specialized fields of study, such as ornithology, and at the same time blurred the lines between science, expertise, and popular culture. Bestiaries, in this capacious sense, were plentiful in the age of empire, embedded as they were in the discursive landscape of exploration, conquest, and administration: activities that constituted the backbone of modern British imperialism's expansive reach and its enduring knowledge regimes. One example is Sir Harry Johnston's *Uganda Protectorate,* a 1904 account of his work as an imperial special commissioner. Over one hundred pages of volume one are dedicated to a chapter on zoology that serves as a minor bestiary, complete with elaborate taxonomical analysis prepared by the eminent professor of natural history and British museum official E. Ray Lankester and overseen by Johnston himself. The full text contains more than five hundred photographs and illustrations, most of them of animals who come in for deep description and what we might call the "imperializing" classification system of natural history. Johnston's narrative serves as a moral tale about evolution and the white man's progress. His expeditionary forces were key to the domestication of a baby elephant they encountered, an animal that the local chiefs had been unable to control. Acknowledging that it was difficult to tame, Johnston was pleased by the results of his "experiments," which turned the young elephant into a "most delightful pet."[5]

It would be easy to take Johnston's proconsular faith in white men's dominion over the animal kingdom as a measure of imperial hubris. Importantly, however, the story of the elephant is followed by an account of the local rhinoceros population, which proved less docile and accommodating than the baby elephant had been. Johnston describes the African rhinoceros as a "blustering creature" and a "grotesque survival from the mammalian epoch." The rhino is a downright nuisance because he routinely engages in "unprovoked charges," goring men before they have a chance to get out of the way. This "unprovoked wrath" was most evident along the Uganda railway lines, where the rhino proved a "dangerous nuisance" to Indian and African workers and especially to British travelers. Johnston's palpable frustration at the capacity of this creature to defy regulation and disrupt imperial transport all at once—and simply because it can—reminds us that animal life, whether large or small, could and did often work against the grain of imperial control. Animals regularly disrupted imperial agendas by defying taxonomies and categories imposed by the British on the natural world. Even when such interruptions were minimal, they represent a challenge to histories of untrammeled species mastery that continue to shape grand narratives of modern British imperialism. By centering animalia, the imperial bestiary points not only to the significance of animals in imperial expansion; it also backlights the instability and vulnerability of empire in ways that cannot be fully appreciated through a focus on the colonizing activity of *Homo imperius* alone.[6]

In *The Order of Things*, in his famous remarks on Borges, Foucault argues that the bestiary is always an arbitrary and highly selective form. What he finds compelling in Borges's efforts to quote a "certain Chinese Encyclopedia" is his attempt to destabilize western systems of classification, an objective that would ultimately inspire Foucault's own writings and lectures. Foucault's interests are in how "our culture has made manifest the existence of order" and which of these "have been recognized, posited, linked with space and time, in order to create the positive basis of knowledge."[7] In other words, Foucault's project is to confront the "order of things" by questioning the ontologies and epistemologies that inform it. Admittedly, by obeying "the alphabetical series (a, b, c, d)," the bestiary that follows may seem to limit the critical potential of Foucault's project by reiterating the familiar hierarchies of language, culture, and civilization that his work has so steadfastly challenged.[8] However, our approach to the making of British imperial histories may also invite other ways to problematize classification schemas. As critics have noted, Foucault did not explicitly question the colonial, racial, or imperial basis of western systems of taxonomy and order.[9] The contributors to this volume extend this project by situating species classification firmly within a dynamic and aspirational British imperial culture, one that projected racial regimes of authority, order, and control by engendering scientific and commonsense knowledges of nature, biology, and species. Among the animals enlisted for this volume, some—like fox or lion—evoke shared European traditions deriving from Aesop and later. Others, including scorpion or ibis, hail particular colonial environments. But the way each creature circulated within and without the spheres of imperial governmentality is typical of how all subjects designated for colonization might at once challenge and elude the grasp of their masters. A combination of iconic and minor figures, the animal species included here are not intended to fully represent empire's symbolic, material, or violent reach. Rather, the alphabetic form allows for juxtapositions that generate unexpected connections. We hope that these may serve as further invitations to rethink the central and often unruly place of animals within British imperial ventures and to conceptualize empire as a multispecies project (for more, see "Some Ways to Read This Book"). The bestiary form is, in this sense, both hybrid and unconventional: neither history nor literature per se, it offers a provocation to new ways of seeing and writing about empire and its biocultural creatures.[10]

To be sure, animals featured prominently in European and non-European empires alike, including the Mughal, Qing, and Egyptian dynasties. What is notable in the Victorian British variant is how imperial authorities and ordinary empire enthusiasts alike drew on animals—as symbols, companions, and machines—to advance projects of would-be imperial extension and consolidation through fictions and fantasies of racial, cultural, and species supremacy. The entries to follow ask questions, trouble, and challenge these assertions in important ways. Together, they illuminate how the ideological and practical contests of empire, which are too often traced only through the archive of human subjects, are thrown into bold relief when explored through animal form. As powerful representations and vehicles for dominion, hegemony, and desire, animals shaped the British imperial imagination in virtually every production it undertook. The British lion symbolized an "interspecies birthright." The imperial raccoon—a transliteration of the Algonquian Powhatan word *arakunem*—came to represent a particular white masculinist "frontier wilderness" that was deeply enmeshed in the racial and colonial violence of Indigenous land appropriations, resource extractions, and African slavery in what is now the United States. Eventually, the raccoon became a symbol of American anti-imperialism, thus proving to be an unstable and disputed marker of British imperial dominance. Animals also signaled the vulnerabilities of empire. Mosquitos, as threats to mammals of various kinds, posed serious challenges to imperial aspirations. Disease outbreaks hindered European control over land and resources but opened possibilities for Indigenous peoples and enslaved Africans—who had immunity—to further resist colonial dominance. By the mid-twentieth century, mosquitoes were commonly used in wartime propaganda to signal the imperial hubris of American power against the alleged racial threat posed by Japanese forces.

Wherever they went, British colonists and emigrants took animals with them, whether as domestic companions, foodstuff, or markers of property and status. The importation of animals formed a central part of the British imperial ethos. In settler colonies including Australia, Canada, and South Africa, animals helped to further Indigenous dispossession by advancing settler claims to landownership through regimes of property, while engendering an accumulation of colonial wealth. But animals were not always obedient companions. New species often devastated local ecologies in settler colonies through deforestation, as in the case of cattle. They also impinged on the subsistence economies of Indigenous peoples and destroyed thriving communities, as evidenced by the wild boar. Native and foreign animals also fought back against pastoral economies and their attendant imaginaries. In the Cape, jackals regularly averted fences and feasted on livestock, thereby threatening the food supplies and property regimes upon which white settler domination relied. The disruptive power of the jackal lay, too, in its relationship to another undesirable, the dingo—so much so that their histories were written as one continuous species (the *Canidae*).[11] In Australia, the red fox—introduced to the colony only so that white settler men could recreate the English foxhunt—became a serious danger to farm animals and to indigenous flora and fauna in ways that both mirror and mimic politically predatory imperial forms. Ivan Kreilkamp has suggested that normative categories like the human, the novel, and the home were all "conceptualized in relation to an animal existence that is at once marginal or excluded but symbolically central and always a shaping influence." If this is so, then empire in all its variations must be considered a major protagonist in the story of how animals came to accrue such imaginative and material power, both at home and "away."[12]

Animals interrupted colonial and imperial projects at every turn. Debates about animal agency are rife in animal studies, inspired in part by Harriet Ritvo's provocation thirty years ago that "animals . . . never talk back" and by new work on the vitalism of nonhuman matter, whether living or not.[13] Contributors to *Animalia* engage the question of animals as actors in a general way; however, our aim is not to attribute intention or will. Rather, we track the trouble that nonhuman creatures of different sorts created for imperial officials, settlers, policies, and ambitions, and the disruptive anti-imperial histories they produced in the process. There are others who share our ABC format and its possibilities in foregrounding the willfulness of creaturely worlds. Hugh Raffles's *Insectopedia* is a marvelous account of the longstanding entanglements between human and insect worlds. "So much about insects is obscure to us," he writes, "yet our capacity to condition their existence is so vast."[14] Weaving between natural science, literature, and philosophy, Raffles documents the porosity of human and insect life, the ways in which humans habituated insects and vice versa. In light of animal studies, in which we include Raffles's compendium, it may seem self-evident to claim that the politics of empire played out in multispecies registers, human/animal, native/foreign, and among species of various kinds. Surprisingly, however, there is still no comprehensive account of how and why this was the case for the modern British Empire, despite the fact that those dynamics can be traced across so many different archives. *Animalia* is not intended to be comprehensive in scope. To paraphrase Raffles, there are just too many animals to include; they are active, indifferent, and always on the move.[15] But even with all its gaps and omissions, *Animalia* offers a sustained discussion of how imperial power was extended through and disrupted by animal species.

One important feature of the bestiary form is that, as a set of short entries, it allows us to see—with particular vividness—just how thoroughly imperial histories have been shaped by nonhuman animals in the Anglophone imperial world. As the essays in this volume show, animal bodies collided with the forces of empire in powerful ways that gave new shape and intensity to the politics of gender, race, sexuality, and class. Hunting offers an obvious example. "The hunt" symbolized the projected racial strength and displayed the material triumphs of empire, and at the same time signaled the vulnerabilities of British imperial manhood. Hunting wild game became a favored pastime for British colonists in the dominions, colonies, and protectorates. If the fox hunt in Australia represented the virtues of the English gentry, the tiger hunt in the forests of South Asia and the whale hunt in the Pacific and Atlantic Oceans were unsurpassed tests of white "manly courage." As a performative conquest over nature, hunting carried other violent effects, as evidenced in the further displacement of Indigenous and tribal peoples from their lands and waterways. Hunting literally gave material flesh to gendered, racial, and class hierarchies along other registers as well. In the imperial metropole, the proceeds of hunting—including whalebones and vulture and kiwi feathers—became highly coveted objects that furnished upscale women's fashion. Animal taxidermy that was proudly displayed in public and private spaces became "physical symbols of the power of the British over colonised lands—and colonised wildlife."[16] Thus, animals and animal parts were status symbols of masculinity, femininity, race, and class mobility through consumption, display, desire, and the relentless quest for military conquest and white settlement. But British consumers witnessed only a small part of hunting that mistakenly signaled the triumph of imperial power. For all the animals killed, many others fought back and escaped. The coveted species of "the hunt" routinely put white British manhood to the test.

Animals signaled inter-imperial contests and connections that were overt and subtle. The British lion and the Russian bear were a common pairing in political iconography, a face-off that signaled imperial rivalries for political and territorial dominance over the Victorian globe. The sacred ibis, a bird that was long revered in Egyptian mythology, newly emerged in nineteenth-century imperial science and spawned a contest between French, British, and American naturalists. Following Napoleon's defeat in Egypt, the mummified bird became "scientific evidence" that ostensibly supported some racial theories of human origins over others. But conflicts between European and Anglo empires were perhaps nowhere more evident than on the high seas. Oceans and continents featured differently in the imperial order of animalia. In the Pacific and Atlantic Oceans, animal species—large and small—crossed jurisdictional divides and dramatized the reality that claims to imperial sovereignty were porous, unstable, and frequently at the mercy of nature. This volume contains two entries on whales (N IS FOR NORTH ATLANTIC RIGHT WHALE and W IS FOR WHALE), each of which points to different ocean regions and to distinct yet shared imperial politics. Whaling in the Atlantic and Pacific tells discrete histories of the animal's significance in Indigenous cosmologies and Anglo-imperial economies and imaginaries. These two entries bring the British and American empires together in ways that foreground competing ambitions over sovereignty and jurisdiction in coastal waters and on the high seas. They also signal the troubled projections of Anglo-imperial control.

Imperial systems of classification were established on an ostensible dividing line that separated humans from animal species. These differentiations are dramatically reflected in the bestiary form, which organizes animals into ascending taxonomies of worth, value and importance. Yet, human/animal distinctions, including their underlying claims to purity, were produced in time, space, and in situ. The lines that divided human from animal were the result of contingencies of time and place that shaped the limits and possibilities of imperial power on the ground and, equally, in the metropolitan imagination. Distinctions between humans and animals, though always informed by assumptions of race and species, were neither static nor stable. In distant colonial outposts and frontiers where European settlement was sparse, white colonists relied heavily on animals for physical and psychic survival. Zebus were crossbred to provide milk, meat, and labor to furnish the material needs of white settlers; dogs offered protection, entertainment, and companionship in foreign and inhospitable environments. Amid the intimacies of human/animal relations, British authorities expressed concerns about other forms of affection that potentially threatened prevailing racial orders. Given that Indigenous and colonial populations were not always regarded to be fully human—and certainly not on equal footing with white Britons—cross-racial desire, many cautioned, was a type of "interspecies" mixing. From the dominions to the colonies, fears of white men "going native" often played out in animal form, as colonial anxieties over the wild boar remind us. Much like European men, feral pigs also broke away from "their domestic enclosures to roam, to prey, and to reproduce" (B IS FOR BOAR). This bestiary seeks to materialize these troublesome and disruptive histories. Imperial narratives of domestication and disorder, we argue, are not often visible in human-centered accounts of British imperial rule.[17]

The bestiary, as this volume makes clear, is a discrete inventory of the British imperial past, and a nod to the present and future as well. In recent years, research in the field of animal studies has expanded in the North American academy and has deepened our appreciation for the permeable boundaries, interconnections, and interdependencies of human and animal life. The study of nonhuman animals has emerged during an extended historical moment that some have called the "Anthropocene," an epoch which signals the devastating effects of human-induced climate change and calls for, among other things, a new set of relationships among humans, animals, and other life forms. As several essays in this volume argue, the transport of animals to different imperial regions, combined with overhunting and overfishing, resulted in the destruction of local ecosystems and the extinction of animal species. The quagga, for instance, which was once indigenous to the Cape, vanished through settler agricultural practices. Whale-hunting in the colonial era significantly depleted the population of North Atlantic right whales, rendering them nearly extinct today. What these animal histories reveal is that the British Empire *must* feature prominently in discussions of the contemporary Anthropocene. British imperial pursuits were among the causes of climate change, though its effects are not often recognized in the crisis of human and nonhuman life or in the future of the planet.

Debates on climate change, which have been shaped in part through the rise of animal studies, need to critically question their own guiding assumptions of species supremacy. The human/animal divide that continues to animate discussions of the Anthropocene today still requires some troubling. The urgencies of planetary destruction demand a better understanding of how human/animal relations have been produced historically, particularly at the high mark of Victorian imperialism, when the British Empire extended control over 85 percent of the world. "Thinking with animals" is perforce an interdisciplinary task to which history is central and a better appreciation of the ideological, symbolic, and material work of empire is indispensable. Despite important case studies that illuminate the centrality of imperial history to animal studies, the latter field has developed mainly out of literary criticism and cultural anthropology. By the same token, British history has yet to grapple fully with imperial biopolitics at multiple scales.[18] *Animalia* works to bring imperial histories to bear more intentionally on emergent conversations about the vibrancy of nonhuman worlds—not only by marking out where animals appear but when, where, and under what conditions they made the project of imperialism more difficult for its agents to accomplish. In that sense, this bestiary works against rather than along the grain of empire history. To the extent possible, it seeks to exceed the "given-ness" of imperial triumph without claiming to fully or finally decolonize.[19] Our emphasis on the disruptive and disorderly force of nonhuman animals is not intended as a triumphalist case for animal resistance. Given the violence to which animals were subject and the extinction rates under global imperial regimes, "agency" must be carefully calibrated. Yet the nonhuman world did pose recurrent challenges to modern British imperialism, interrupting the best-made plans and reminding would-be colonizers on a regular basis that the terrains they sought to conquer were not uninhabited but were populated both by humans and by unruly animal species that refused to go away.

As with any classification system, our ABC is not comprehensive, nor is it intended to be. Such a survey is likely the work of a lifetime, and in this digital age may be a project best achieved beyond the confines of a single book between two covers. The sheer vastness of a multispecies world that the forces of British imperialism struggled with and against suggests the limits of linearity and narrative coherence when it comes to telling anti-imperial animal histories. Though this volume is far from an encyclopedic account, each bestiary letter does more than represent a single animal artefact or tell a cohesive animal story. It serves as what Sara Ahmed calls an orientation device, aimed at uncovering different genealogies of how racialized imperial supremacy took shape in Anglophone cultural production over the last 150 years.[20] These processes were not static, nor were they solely human. They were the site of imperial power and anticolonial struggle represented potently in and through the forms and forces of entangled human/animal worlds. The illustrations that accompany each letter reveal the ways in which interspecies relations were indispensable in British claims to racial superiority—and Indigenous/colonial inferiority—precisely through the relationality and interdependence of the "human" and the "animal." This dynamic might be called "mutual ecologies," a term coined by the primatologist Augustin Fuentes.[21] The entanglements of human and animal worlds is so broad and so deep that animal scholars speak of the codevelopment or coevolution of the horse or the dog and the historical human over wide swaths of time.[22] Nonhuman animals also share intertwined histories, as the okapi, with its links to the equine, the giraffid, and even the mythic unicorn suggests. These genus histories and the social, cultural, and economic conditions that produced them extend, in some cases, from the ancient world to the present. For practical purposes, we focus more narrowly on the British Empire from the 1850s to the post–World War I period, though some of the contributors reach further back and forward in time as a way to highlight specific patterns and developments. As an entry point into more-than-human imperial worlds, we hope that this book will provoke reflections on the bestiaries still to be excavated from other colonial histories, contexts and empires.

Finally, *Animalia* is an imperial bestiary and an archive of anti-imperial histories. Conventional imperial histories are themselves a genre framed by colonizer-colonized models that emphasize extension, hegemony, and settlement over the persistently troubled ground of empire's lived reality.[23] This is not the same as a chronicle of imperial criticism of the kind attributed, say, to Edward Lear for the "anticolonial bestiary" of his animal limericks.[24] Nor is it equivalent to arguing that the boundaries that might be said to distinguish the domestic from the wild, or the colonial subject from the colonial animal, were constantly blurred (though they often were). What the texts and images that follow illuminate—with startling variety and consistency—is the concerted *attempt* to legitimate the supremacy of *Homo sapiens* (often as white and male bodies) through a symbolic and material mastery over animals across the many territories of imperial dominion, and the recurrent *limits* placed on those efforts by a variety of nonhuman animals. Even when these limits appear as minor or insignificant, they signal the vulnerability of the imperial project to a variety of antagonists: humans, nonhuman animals, and combinations thereof. As with all histories of imperial power—and despite the savagery and violence its agents wrought—the real story is in the struggle over whether and to what extent such supremacy was actually achieved. *Animalia* offers a multispecies archive of the aspirations for human dominance that underwrote the British imperial enterprise, and how the "natural world" and its denizens challenged these claims on various scales. The animal archives pieced together here expose the uneven and contested ground of species ambition, and with it the drag on notions of unqualified imperial "success" that animal forms exercised in the realm of representation and cultural production. The combination of texts and images suggests the histories of contradiction and instability that a catalogue of imperial animals has the potential to materialize. Readers might approach the book as an unruly taxonomy that works at odd angles, through idiosyncrasies, and across historical and geographical storylines in ways that open new juxtapositions and conversations (see more in "Some Ways to Read this Book").

That searing critiques of the limits of the human are unfolding today—alongside the ongoing struggles of Indigenous peoples, descendants of African slaves, and the formerly colonized who are fighting, even now, to be recognized as human—deserves some serious consideration. That such a contradiction should manifest at a moment of historically unprecedented neo-imperialism on a global scale is remarkable, yet little remarked on. *Animalia* represents a particular kind of archive of imperial and racial thinking that reflects how human species supremacy was asserted through struggles over nature, including efforts to dominate and domesticate animals in the modern British Empire. By making a case for the urgency of visualizing that contest now, as we confront ongoing struggles for social and racial justice against the threat of planetary extinction, we offer this bestiary as a historical intervention into a contemporary moment, fixed resolutely on the present and the future. If the ABC appears to be an elementary form that seems easy to apprehend, the anti-imperial bestiary is a mode of reading that is opposed and antagonistic to the protocols of conventional empire history. It is a reminder of how powerfully genres of representation and forms of narrative matter in how we understand the entanglement of human/animal worlds, imperial ambitions, and the horizon of planetary life itself.

Notes

1 Deborah Denenholz Morse and Martin Danahay, eds., *Victorian Animal Dreams: Representations of Animals in Victorian Literature and Culture* (Aldershot, UK: Ashgate, 2007).

2 Diana Donald, *Picturing Animals in Britain, 1750–1850* (New Haven, CT: Yale University Press, 2008).

3 Richard Owen, *Memoir on the Gorilla* (London: Taylor and Francis, 1865). For fiction, see John Miller, *Empire and the Animal Body: Violence, Identity and Ecology in Victorian Adventure Fiction* (London: Anthem, 2012).

4 John Lockwood Kipling, *Beast and Man in India: A Popular Sketch of Indian Animals in Their Relations with the People* (London: Macmillan, 1892).

5 Sir Harry Johnston, *The Uganda Protectorate* (London: Hutchison, 1904), 1:371. See also E. Ray Lankester, *The History and Scope of Zoology* (New York: Humboldt, 1892).

6 Johnston, *Uganda Protectorate*, xx. For a luminous reflection on how Victorian pets backlight this generalized precarity in a rapidly industrializing—and, I would add, imperializing—world, see Teresa Mangum, "Animal Angst: Victorians Memorialize Their Pets," in *Victorian Animal Dreams*, ed. Morse and Danahay, 15–34.

7 Michel Foucault, *The Order of Things: An Archaeology of Human Sciences* (London: Routledge, 2002), xxiii.

8 Foucault, *Order of Things*, xvii.

9 For a critique of Foucault's lack of attention to colonialism and racism see Ann Laura Stoler, *Race and the Education of Desire: Foucault's History of Sexuality and the Colonial Order of Things* (Durham, NC: Duke University Press, 1995).

10 Here we borrow from Samantha Frost's evocative title, *Biocultural Creatures: Toward a New Theory of the Human* (Durham, NC: Duke University Press, 2016).

11 St. George Jackson Mivart, *Dogs, Jackals, Wolves and Foxes: Monograph of the Canidae* (London: Taylor and Francis, 1890).

12 Ivan Kreilkamp, *Minor Creatures: Persons, Animals and the Victorian Novel* (Chicago: University of Chicago Press, 2018), 1–2.

13 Harriet Ritvo, *The Animal Estate: The English and Other Creatures in the Victorian Age* (Cambridge, MA: Harvard University Press, 1987), 5.

See also Erica Fudge, *Animal* (London: Reaktion, 2002). On the new
materialisms, see Diana Coole and Samantha Frost, eds., *New Materialisms: Ontologies, Agency, and Politics* (Durham, NC: Duke University
Press, 2010); *Social Text* ("Interspecies," special issue edited by Julie
Livingston and Jasbir K. Puar) 29, 1 (Spring 2011). The challenges here
are epistemological as well as ontological; as Walter Johnson shows,
in some historical and historiographical contexts the very definition
of agency is bound up with the striving to "preserve humanity." See
Walter Johnson, "On Agency," *Journal of Social History* 37, 1 (2003):
114.

14 Hugh Raffles, *Insectopedia* (New York: Random House, 2010), 44.

15 Raffles, *Insectopedia*, 4.

16 Alice Would, "The Curious Creatures of Victorian Taxidermy," *History Today*, July 4, 2018. https://www.historytoday.com/alice-would
/curious-creatures-victorian-taxidermy.

17 For a different example of the abecedarium, see Antoinette Burton,
ed., *An ABC of Queen Victoria's Empire; or, A Primer of Conquest, Dissent
and Disruption* (London: Bloomsbury, 2017).

18 Lorraine Daston and Gregg Mittman, eds., *Thinking with Animals: New
Perspectives on Anthropomorphism* (New York: Columbia University
Press, 2005). For examples of such case studies, one well established
and two more recent, see John McNeil, *Mosquito Empires: Ecology and
War in the Greater Caribbean* (Cambridge, UK: Cambridge University
Press, 2010); Julie E. Hughes, *Animal Kingdoms: Hunting, the Environment and Power in the Indian Princely States* (Cambridge, MA: Harvard
University Press, 2013); James Hevia, *Animal Labor and Colonial War-
fare* (Chicago: University of Chicago Press, 2018). For an astute assess-
ment of the prospects of animal histories in the age of empire, see
Jonathan Saha, "Among the Beasts of Burma: Animals and the Politics
of Colonial Sensibilities, c. 1840–1940," *Journal of Social History* 48, 4
(2015): 912–13; Kathleen Kete, ed., *A Cultural History of Animals in the
Age of Empire* (London: Bloomsbury, 2008).

19 For one discussion of the stakes of these methodological challenges,
see Billy-Ray Belcourt, "Animal Bodies, Colonial Subjects: (Re)Locat-
ing Animality in Decolonial Thought," *Societies* 5, 1 (2015): 1–11.

20 Sara Ahmed, *Queer Phenomenology: Orientations, Objects, Others* (Durham, NC: Duke University Press, 2006).

21 Cited in Jane Desmond, *Displaying Death and Animating Life: Human-
Animal Relations in Art, Science, and Everyday Life* (Chicago: University
of Chicago Press, 2016), 21.

22 Elaine Walker, *Horse* (London: Reaktion, 2008), 12; Edmund Russell,
Greyhound Nation: A Coevolutionary History of England, 1200–1900
(Cambridge, UK: Cambridge University Press, 2018).

23 See Antoinette Burton, *The Trouble with Empire: Challenges to Modern British Imperialism* (Oxford: Oxford University Press, 2015).

24 Ann C. Colley, "Edward Lear's Anti-Colonial Bestiary," *Victorian Poetry* 30, 2 (1992): 109–20.

SOME WAYS TO READ
THIS BOOK

—

Intuitively, perhaps, we read books from cover to cover. A bestiary certainly encourages this, with the momentum of the ABC format propelling us forward from beginning to end. Readers may well start this book with Ape and end with Zebu. If they do, they will jump straight into Darwinian debates about the species boundary (and, by extension, into the racialization of simian forms) and end up in an account of the global-imperial dispersion of the zebu (and, by extension, its role in cow protection agitation under the Raj).

Yet it's also possible to read this book in other directions, to dip in and out by following the cross-referencing we have embedded within the text (see also C IS FOR CATTLE and Z IS FOR ZEBU). There are untold connections that will come to mind by moving from back to front or from the middle outward—or by simply sampling entries randomly, when an image or category strikes the reader. Reading against the linearity and forward momentum of the ABC offers an invitation to imagine the British Empire along different coordinates and scales. From a multispecies vantage point that centers animal archives, terrains of empire look more like assemblages replete with depths and widths than flat cartographies color coded as sovereign territories. Reading this way also generates possibilities for new configurations of time, space, and boundaries. R IS FOR RACCOON, for example, pulls us from British colonial America to John Bull and Abraham Lincoln via the work of *Punch* illustrator John Tenniel. What this and several other entries point to are the multispecies dimensions of imperial geographies, and how animal charisma illuminates the biopolitics of colonial "possession."

Quintessentially didactic, the bestiary format is a multipurpose teaching tool, if an unconventional one. Whether you take a linear or an animal-hopping approach, students have the opportunity to grasp what the creaturely worlds of empire look like and how they structured imperial politics, cultures, and imagination. Each contributor "reads" the image in the text, highlighting the dynamic, uncertain, and potentially disruptive role of animals in imperial politics and illustrating the various points at which the human mastery of empire reached its limits. Each entry ends with an alternative list of other possible animal-letter combinations. This serves as an invitation to consider potential building blocks for additional bestiaries. Such an assignment immerses students in deep empirical detail, in synthetic case-making around a specific animal, in the visual universe of imperial print culture, and in the challenges of narrating empire histories that question imperial assumptions and protocols of representation. It presents a graphic exercise that lends itself to digital technologies as well as more familiar textual iterations. A serious intellectual enterprise that communicates its knowledge accessibly, this bestiary rests on a scholarly apparatus but is not weighed down by it; hence the modest suggestions for further readings rather than a full catalog of citations and attributions. As the introduction suggests, *Animalia* is not intended to be a comprehensive archive of modern British imperial creatures but, rather, a primer for how to examine imperial power through nonhuman animal worlds.

Creating new bestiaries out of *Animalia* is an uncanny echo of nineteenth-century British reading practices. These practices emphasized readers as active participants in and producers of the texts they read and assumed that the reading experience itself resulted in part from a combination of content and form. The bestiary that we present here, including the multiple itineraries that readers can follow, encourages novel ways to problematize and reconceptualize the human/animal divide and to question the species distinctions among animals. Whether it is Darwin's head atop an ape's body (A IS FOR APE) or half-Afghan, half-scorpion creatures scrambling around John Bull's feet (S IS FOR SCORPION), the bestiary's visual archive shows how entangled and interdependent these ecologies were.

By offering an entrée into empire on a microscale, the "small histories" afforded by each letter may make "big history" seem more accessible. Perhaps more importantly, the microscale along which *Animalia* is written opens alternative archives from which to study imperial power—archives that may break down what are often false dichotomies between big and small, local and global histories. In an age of TLDR ("too long, didn't read"), the bestiary is one of the more malleable genres available for keeping history dynamic and, in this case, for thinking critically about the field of imperial power. It is especially useful for generating debates about who the agents of empire were and how we render them as antecedents to the present. As we note in the introduction, these questions take on a particular urgency in our current historical moment of climate catastrophe and human-induced climate change. Today, we are witnessing not only the extinction of particular animal species (the North Atlantic right whale and the quagga, for example) but also the destruction of planetary life as we know it. As many critics have noted, the responsibility for climate change cannot be evenly distributed across the globe. Discussions of the Anthropocene often have a presentist focus, which willfully ignores the effects of the European and U.S. empires and the role of territorial expansion, dispossession, and extraction in the destruction of the planet. In the interests of global capitalism and European racial supremacy, imperial powers have violently altered local ecologies in ways that we are only seeing with clarity now. *Animalia* gives readers a longer historical arc in which to situate and consider these contemporary urgencies—and a chance to assess the role of global imperialism in the making of our collective future, a future that can only be multispecies.

A

is for

APE

While the word conjures images of majestic silverback gorillas, an ape is not exactly an animal. It is a category, a taxonomical descriptor. As early as the medieval period, "ape" referred to any number of simians. Eventually, early modern zoology specified that apes were monkeys without tails, notably orangutans, chimpanzees, and gorillas. Pre-Darwinian zoologists often represented apes as more human and hence in opposition to monkeys. Therefore, an ape can be multiple, very different species. While the scientific use of "ape" became more specific, popular uses of "ape" (also originating in the Middle Ages) persisted. An ape is a person who imi-

....

"A Venerable Orang-Outang," drawing of Charles Darwin as an ape. From *The Hornet*, March 22, 1871. Source: UCL Library Services Galton Papers 3.

tates another, often in a vulgar or obvious way, and the verb "to ape" captures the action of such mimicry. The history of the word demonstrates that it is riven with troubling ambiguity. Well before Darwinian evolutionary theory, the simian, both real and imaginary, confounded a series of stable boundaries fundamental to modernity—demarcations between species, between the human and the nonhuman, and between the claim to the originary and its imitations.

Apes became more central to Victorian public discourse in what was arguably the greatest Anglo-American controversy of the nineteenth century: Darwin's publication of the *Origin of Species* in 1859 and then *Descent of Man* in 1871, and the subsequent public debate over his claim that humans and apes shared a common ancestor. Darwinian evolutionary theory became widely accepted as scientific fact. Simultaneously, his arguments connecting humans and apes were misrepresented, refuted, and mocked in British popular culture. Upon the publication of *Descent of Man*, cartoons appeared in comedic weekly magazines and interrogated evolutionary claims through a series of encounters between apes and men. One such cartoon, published in 1871 in the *Hornet* magazine, creates a hybrid creature with the head of Darwin on the body of an orangutan. These images sometimes constituted a challenge to the claim that Darwin was the first and only scientist to develop the theory of evolution and natural selection. Other images contested the claim of an evolutionary link between humans and apes. Consistently, though, in every picture, the boundary between the human and the nonhuman is undone.

However transformative the paradigm shift caused by Darwin's work, it existed in a much longer continuum of representations of the simian, and apes in particular. The unsettling, even uncanny relationship between humans and apes circulated in European discourse and experience well before 1859. For example, the word "orangutan" appears to be a translation of the Malay word for "wild man." This uneasy relationship between humans and apes figures even in scientific knowledge. Following the work of early modern anatomists and naturalists who visited Africa or who encountered apes brought back to Europe by early colonial travelers, Carl Linnaeus classified humans and apes in the same taxon in his 1735 *Systema Naturæ*. In editions of his taxonomy published for over thirty years, humans and apes were identified as "Anthropomorpha," which can be translated as "like humans" or "having human form." This was eventually replaced by the category of "primates." Thus, the emergence of biological taxonomy already shows a scientific insistence on the similarities between human beings and apes.

In British popular culture throughout the eighteenth and nineteenth centuries, representations of apes manifested this doubleness. Travel narratives emphasized apes' human characteristics: they were described as expressing human emotions, as having the face of a man, and as performing certain tasks that most animals did not. In writings about animals on exhibit, Britons saw themselves in apes, particularly those that were caught, transported, and put on display in zoos. In 1837, one of many orangutans captured in Angola and Borneo and brought to England was visited by Charles Darwin in the London Zoo. He declared the ape, named Jenny, to be "like a naughty child," and he meticulously recorded her human attributes. Five years later, Queen Victoria visited another orangutan in the London Zoo and wrote in her diary of watching the creature drink tea: "He is frightful & painfully and disagreeably human." This slippery and unsettling relationship between human and ape was also reflected in the way that apes figured in the emerging pseudoscience of racial anthropology. From the beginning, so-called explorers represented apes as on a racial continuum with Africans. Thus, the ape became a vehicle through which to express colonial racism. In his 1718 account of his voyage to Borneo, British explorer Daniel Beeckman describes an encounter with an "Oran-Ootan" and describes him as "handsomer I am sure than some Hottentots I have seen." This marriage between naturalism and racism was more fully theorized in the work of racial scientists such as Georges Cuvier, who argued not only that apes and humans were separately created but that Africans and Asians might share ancestry with apes that Europeans did not. He most famously studied Saartjie Baartman, the South African woman and slave whose body was displayed throughout Europe as a racial curiosity and spectacle in circuses. Cuvier and his colleagues described Baartman's body as apelike and as evidence of how African people were closer anatomically to orangutans than to Europeans. The case of Baartman serves as an egregious example of how apes figured regularly in racist discourse and practices, in particular as a way to assert European superiority and the supposed inferiority of colonized peoples. Apes could call attention to a troubling kinship between human and animals; they also served both to invoke and reject a troubling common humanity between colonizer and colonized, between slave owner and slave. The domination of colonized peoples was often legitimized through the use of an evolutionary scale of humanity and racist associations between the colonized and apes.

Indeed, nineteenth-century degeneration theories explored categories of European people, in particular criminals and the insane, who were understood to have devolved in an evolutionary and sociopolitical sense from the standard of European "civilization." Robert Louis Stevenson's *Dr. Jekyll and Mr. Hyde* stands as the most widely read literary work that explores the paradoxes concerning degeneration. Dr. Jekyll's "ape-like" double, whose difference is marked in particular by his "hairy hand," stands as an abstract representation of all that is "primitive" within the bachelor doctor, simultaneously residing within the human and exteriorized from it. Here, the ape serves as a kind of monstrous vessel that performs the work of exploring and managing a wide range of anxieties—about criminality, "uncivilized" psychic states, sexuality, including queer desire, bourgeois masculinity, and the violence and amorality of animals and humans alike. Stevenson's ubiquitous novel stands as a reminder that a menacing animal threat lurked within all humans and their psyches. By 1888, the first newspaper stories about "Jack the Ripper" referred readers to *Jekyll and Hyde*. In sensation journalism, the literary narrative of the simian lurking within us became the key to understanding the monstrous criminal lurking among the public.

Apes demarcated that which threatened the human and middle-class European values in terrifying ways. In particular after Darwin, apes were represented in travel, naturalist, and literary narratives as violent, powerful, destructive, villainous, and preternaturally strong. Over the course of the nineteenth century and into the twentieth, new literary and cultural forms allowed for the dissemination of gothic stories of apes. Young boys read adventures such as R.M. Ballantyne's very popular *The Gorilla Hunters: A Tale of the Wilds of Africa*. Ballantyne's novel was contemporaneous with and likely influenced by the anthropological writings and public lectures of celebrity explorer Paul Du Chaillu. Du Chaillu returned from his travels throughout equatorial Africa with gorilla skulls and taxidermied gorillas that he displayed while lecturing. These collected samples were used as evidence by racial anthropologists and those engaging in debates about Darwinian evolutionary theory. Du Chaillu disseminated gorillas into the popular imagination through his travel narratives, such as *Explorations and Adventures in Equatorial Africa*, and a collection of children's stories, *Sto-*

ries of the Gorilla Country, both written in 1861. Later, imperial gothic novels such as Rider Haggard's *Allan Quatermain* trilogy represented their heroes as facing the attack of gigantic gorillas. These novels stand within an archive of colonial texts featuring alarming apes, from Edgar Rice Burroughs's Tarzan novels, first published in 1912, to the first King Kong movie made in 1933. In these texts and others—such as the infamous 1902 short story "The Monkey's Paw," by W. W. Jacobs—the ape (and monkeys more broadly) represents Indigenous knowledge and power in the form of anticolonial violence, alternative political structures such as matriarchy, and the supernatural. Apes also represented the threat of uncontrollable nature in regions of Africa and Asia, and the dangers posed when that nature, incapable of domestication, was brought "home" to Europe. In fact, in what is arguably the first piece of detective fiction, "The Murders in the Rue Morgue," written in 1841 by Edgar Allan Poe, the brutal murderer of two women is revealed to be an orangutan brought to Paris from Borneo by a sailor. The ape stood as both an object of pity and an agent of "savage" violence, and critics often read the story as expressing complex anxieties about slave rebellion in the United States. In one of the text's most famous scenes, the orangutan is discovered trying to shave, suggesting the threat that the ape might cross over or even pass as human. Later, in 1891's "Bertran and Bimi," Rudyard Kipling inaugurates a genre that persists today: the tale of the ape that is introduced into the bourgeois family and transitions from pet to child. This story, like those that follow it, ends in inevitable brutal violence and serves as a cautionary tale about mistaking the ape for the human.

Victorian visual culture further explored the connections between apes and violence as revolutionary, and insurgent violence as explicitly simian. The iconography of revolutionaries as angry apes first appeared in late eighteenth-century British reactions to both the French Revolution and the rebellion of the United Irishmen nine years later. The counterrevolutionary caricatures of James Gillray drew physiognomic connections between Jacobins, English rioters, and Irish republicans by simianizing them, giving them what L. Perry Curtis has called the "prognathous features" associated with apes. Over the course of the nineteenth century, a tradition of cartoon art emerged in which Irish insurgents in particular were represented as apes. These images used the ape to delegitimize Irish anticolonial politics; resistance to colonial domination is recast as an expression of animal violence and racial atavism. The human aspects of the ape are transformed into the apelike aspects of the human, in particular the colonial subject who is deemed racially inferior. Colonial modernity is not disrupted by resistance to injustice and exploitation but by the very nature of those who refuse to be incorporated into the civilizing mission. As Irish people who participated in anticolonial movements were understood as apes, they were cast outside of the fold of the human. Therefore, these simian representations justified counterinsurgent violence and the suspension of fundamental rights such as habeas corpus. If rebels' actions were understood, like mob violence, as the absence of human rationality and as the outburst of the ape's viciousness, then they must be stopped at all costs. These cartoons often mobilized gendered narratives of feminine vulnerability: the Irish ape-man, representing anticolonial insurgency, frightens a maidenlike Hibernia, figure of the innocent population of Ireland. If the ape was both strangely human and inhumanely brutal, this also implied that the human might easily become monstrously animal or has an apelike side that could emerge unexpectedly.

Both the material and narrative history of the ape bring into stark relief the contradictory impulses of humanization and dehumanization in the project of empire. Who counted as human would have potentially catastrophic consequences in the colonial contest. The ape continually marked the porous and mutable boundaries between colonizer and colonized; between those understood as a population to be managed through domination or bureaucratic rule and those who claimed the right to power; and between those whose violence was rationalized as a form of progress and those whose resistance was racialized and deemed a vestige of the ape in humankind.

Suggestions for Further Reading

Beer, Gillian. *Darwin's Plots: Evolutionary Narrative in Darwin, George Eliot and Nineteenth Century Fiction*. 3rd ed. Cambridge, UK: Cambridge University Press, 1992, 2009.

Brown, Laura. *Homeless Dogs and Melancholy Apes: Humans and Other Animals in the Modern Literary Imagination*. Ithaca, NY: Cornell University Press, 2010.

Conniff, Richard. *The Species Seekers: Heroes, Fools, and the Mad Pursuit of Life on Earth*. New York: Norton, 2011.

Curtis, L. P. *Apes and Angels: The Irishman in Victorian Caricature*. Rev. ed. Washington, DC: Smithsonian Institution Press, 1997.

Danahay, Martin. "Dr. Jekyll's Two Bodies." *Nineteenth Century Contexts* 35, 1 (2013): 23–40.

McCook, Stuart. "'It May Be Truth, but It Is Not Evidence': Paul Du Chaillu and the Legitimation of Evidence in the Field Sciences." *Osiris* 11 (1996): 177–97.

Pollock, Mary Sanders. *Storytelling Apes: Primatology Narratives Past and Present*. University Park: Pennsylvania State University Press, 2015.

Richter, Victoria. *Literature after Darwin: Human Beasts in Western Fiction, 1859–1939*. New York: Palgrave Macmillan, 2011.

Sax, Boria. "Monkeys and Apes, an Essay in Pictures." *Huffington Post*, March 11, 2014. https://www.huffpost.com/entry/monkeys-and-apes -an-essay_b_4934167.

Stevenson, Robert Louis. *The Strange Case of Dr. Jekyll and Mr. Hyde*. 3rd ed. Edited by Martin Danahay. Peterborough, ON: Broadview, 2015.

A is also for...

Aardvark
Albatross
Alligator
Antelope
Armadillo

is for

BOAR

Almost anywhere one went in the vast territories of the British Empire, one was likely to find boar. Whether domestic pigs that went feral or an indigenous population of *Sus scrofa*, boar were everywhere, and they were both a boon and a plague. An indispensable ally to the settler, they provided a ready and a plentiful source of food. They were also a powerful foe, threatening livestock, crops, ecosystems, and even politics and people. Boar seemed to both undermine and advance empire at every cloven-hoofed step, a contradictory status that sprang from their huge appetites, their fierce tempers, and their prodigious fertility.

Sus scrofa, or wild boar, became *Sus scrofa domesticus*, or domestic pigs, several times over from Southeast Asia to the Middle East between eleven thousand and six thousand years ago. Wild or domestic, all male pigs are boars. In urban areas, these omnivorous scavengers devoured human waste (everything from offal to the refuse of outhouses). On rural farms, they could be set loose to forage in the forests, to be called up (or hunted down) whenever pork was required. But domestic pigs were always just a hair's breadth away, it seemed, from returning

....

Thomas Lempriere, untitled sketch of piggeries at convict settlement at Macquarie Harbour. From *Sketchbook of Drawings, Mainly of Macquarie Harbour, No. 5*, ca. 1828. Courtesy of State Library of Tasmania.

to their wild origins. Highly intelligent and very strong, they escape easily from fences and other enclosures and head for the hills, the forest, or the rivers. Given any adequate food source, boar populations will explode quickly and exponentially, because sows produce litters every four months. Wherever pigs were brought to feed humans, wild boar became a problem—one made all the worse by their famously bad tempers, razor-sharp tusks, cunning, speed, and power. Everywhere they were penned up, pigs broke loose and went feral, wandering forests and fields, despoiling landscapes, and provoking the neighbors. In Australia and New Zealand, as elsewhere, they tore down fences, devoured crops and eggs, and preyed on young lambs. They rampaged through native estuaries, consuming huge quantities of mollusks, shellfish, and all parts of native plants including the fruit, seeds, roots, bulbs, tubers, and foliage. They simultaneously undermined both the pastoral economy of the settlers and the subsistence harvests of Indigenous people, making wild boar a point of contention for everyone. Colonial newspapers were filled with horror stories of farmers who were killed or maimed by boars, or who lost their children to animals on the rampage. In New Zealand, feral pigs—known as "Captain Cookers," after the navigator who introduced them—became such a problem in the 1860s that bounties of six pence apiece were offered for their tails.

Boar became especially troublesome on islands throughout the Atlantic and Pacific Oceans. Explorers, whalers, sealers, and deep-sea fishermen—the front lines of an expanding maritime empire—all dropped off pairs of breeding boars and sows on islands as a kind of insurance policy against shipwreck. Their notorious seasickness and aversion to water meant that boars became a favorite talismanic tattoo, a protection against drowning in use well into the twentieth century: "pig on the knee, safety at sea." But their name was still taboo at sea and had to be replaced by words like "Curly-Tail" or Turf-Rooter." The latter epithet also described what hogs did to their new island homes. In their relentless search for food above and below ground, boars left destruction in their wake, tearing up and irreparably damaging natural ecosystems.

Boar may have been threatening and destructive, but that didn't change the fact that colonies needed swine flesh. For those who ate pork (a practice that cleaved imperial subjects along religious lines), pigs not only consumed but also produced a prodigious amount of food, in a stunning number of varieties—bacon, ham, sausages, roasts, and salt pork, among others. The possession of a piggery was an essential step in rendering a foreign landscape familiar, a means to gain a foothold in even the most hostile and forbidding places, to establish continuity of foodways between Europe and the colonies. Imperial cookbooks like Edward Abbott's 1864 *English and Australian Cookery Book* invited white settler gourmands to replicate the pork roasts of home, alongside feasts of kangaroo tail and wallaby roast. But as in so many other cases, the idyll of colonial domesticity was paper-thin and precarious. In 1828, the naturalist Thomas Lempriere sketched the pig enclosure at Macquarie Harbour, a convict settlement on the exposed western shore of Van Diemen's Land (Tasmania). The image of industrious convicts laboring peacefully in a pastoral settlement is nearly obscured by water damage and dirt, on pages yellowed by years in a harsh climate. The stains speak to the deeper truth of the image. Macquarie Harbour was no pastoral paradise. It was a site of "secondary punishment," described by nineteenth-century historian John West as "sacred to the genius of torture," and by contemporary historian Hamish Maxwell-Stewart as "a place of exile within a land of exile, a prison within a prison." While the pigs roamed the deep woods of the Western Wilderness, gorging on native orchid roots, the male and female convicts sentenced to Macquarie Harbour were penned up and subjected to often sadistic punishment. Eventually, the pigs were also caught and fed on grass; not long after Lempriere sketched them, they starved to death.

Salt pork was especially crucial to the survival of new settler colonies, especially when both traditional owners and the land itself rejected invaders. The early years of the Australian penal colonies were marked by intense food insecurity, as the colonies could not sustain themselves or the constant influx of convicts from Britain. For a time, New South Wales became dependent on salt pork from Tahiti, a trade that transformed the Polynesian breed of *Sus scrofa* and the roles that pigs played in culture and society. Like their later European counterparts, Polynesian navigators brought pigs with them on their outrigger canoes on great voyages across the Pacific. In Hawai'i and Tahiti, as elsewhere, pigs became central to cultural life as "good food for gods and men," important gifts that maintained or restored the balance between ordinary people, rulers, gods and the environment. The boar was also the chosen *ata* (embodiment) of the god 'Oro, who became the paramount god in Tahiti and Ra'iatea in the eighteenth century, when he adopted his warrior form of 'Oro-taua. When domestic boars suddenly turned violent, it was a "sign that the mouth of 'Oro was open ready to consume the chief and his clans." The Tahitian trade in pigs and salt pork to colonists, whalers, and sealers sustained Britain's Australian penal colonies, the global whaling industry, and the trade in sealskins to China (see N IS FOR NORTH ATLANTIC RIGHT WHALE and W IS FOR WHALE). Boars were transformed into currency, altering both the ecology of the islands and their politics. This changed the status of chiefs and their relationships with commoners and the outside world, and changed the boar themselves, as they interbred with European pigs to become fatter, bigger, and more aggressive.

Boar routinely unnerved—and quite literally unmanned—imperial men, from settler-farmers to big game hunters. In Britain, the nobility's pursuit of boar as a worthy foe in battle had wiped the species out by the sixteenth century. But in the colonies, especially in India, "pig-sticking" was a popular blood sport, with very different, yet linked, meanings for British and Indian elite. In both cases, the physical prowess demonstrated in the boar hunt was a prerequisite for rule. For the British, the blood sport of pig-sticking self-consciously mimicked the medieval boar hunt that had rousted the animals from Britain in the first place. Colonial pig-sticking was supposed to be a proxy for fox-hunting, requiring horses, dogs, and a spear to dispatch an enraged, tusked boar. It was a sport that traveled with British men as they careered around the empire, from New Zealand to India to South Africa and beyond, resulting in a number of late-nineteenth-century memoirs with titles like *Reminiscences of Twenty Years' Pigsticking in Bengal*. R. S. S. Baden-Powell, the founder of the Boy Scouts, called it a health-giving pursuit that honed horsemanship and prepared cavalry officers for combat in a future European conflict. As the historian John Mackenzie has pointed out, Baden-Powell and others saw pig-sticking as "an emblem of the moral force of imperialism, vanquishing the darker forces of an outer world, as well as representing an act of protection by the rulers on behalf of the ruled." At least, that is, until the ruled got themselves gored. A *Punch* illustration from 1878 illustrated this perfectly. The Viceroy of India, Lord Lytton, is depicted as an enthusiastic British pig-sticker being unhorsed by an escaping Afghan boar, surrounded by the tracks of a Russian bear at the height of the Great Game and the second Afghan War. For the Rajput princes whom British civil servants emulated, however, the boar hunt meant something quite different. It was an assertion of sovereignty and continuity with the past, an expression of princely authority over territory and animals, a means to emphasize a maharaja's defense of his people and their livelihoods, and a way to cement alliances with nobles. For Rajput princes, killing boar was a prerequisite for entering manhood—and the failures of British officers and civil servants to live up to this ideal made them ripe for mockery. Comic depictions of hapless and trembling British officials being unseated, intimidated, and gored by wild boars decorated private murals in the Rajput palace of Nahar Odi, a spectacle of schadenfreude for the amusement of the maharaja and his nobles in the late nineteenth century.

Colonial anxiety about wild boars seems like a mirror of deep-seated colonial fears about men "going native" on far-flung foreign shores, breaking out of their domestic enclosures to roam, prey, and reproduce. It also seemed to reflect the profound hubris of colonial exploits, from exploration to settlement. The boar-pig extended the global expansion of empire, providing a steady source of food on the hoof or in the pork barrel. But at the same time, the destructiveness and fierceness of the boar (wild or domestic) was a constant reminder of the tenuous foothold of British settlement in the face of tenacious opposition from both Indigenous people and environments.

Suggestions for Further Reading

Abbott, Edward. *The English and Australian Cookery Book: For the Many, as Well as for the "Upper Ten Thousand."* London: Sampson Low, Son, and Marston, 1864.

Baden-Powell, R.S.S. *Pigsticking; or, Hoghunting: A Complete Account for Sportsmen, and Others.* Pall Mall, UK: Harrison, 1889. http://hdl .handle.net/2027/uc2.ark:/13960/t5j962d35.

Beahrs, Andrew. "Slush on the Mizzentops, Butter in the Hold: Food on American Clipper Ships." *Gastronomica* 12, 4 (2012): 37–45.

Boyce, James. *Van Diemen's Land*, Melbourne: Black, Inc., 2010.

Essig, Mark. *Lesser Beasts: A Snout-to-Tail History of the Humble Pig.* New York: Basic Books, 2015.

Goldberg-Hiller, Jonathan, and Noenoe K. Silva. "Sharks and Pigs: Animating Hawaiian Sovereignty against the Anthropological Machine." *South Atlantic Quarterly* 110, 2 (2011): 429–46.

Hughes, Julie E. *Animal Kingdoms: Hunting, the Environment, and Power in the Indian Princely States*. Cambridge, MA: Harvard University Press, 2013.

MacKenzie, John. *The Empire of Nature: Hunting, Conservation, and British Imperialism*. Manchester, UK: Manchester University Press, 1988.

Newell, Jennifer. *Trading Nature: Tahitians, Europeans, and Ecological Exchange*. Honolulu: University of Hawai'i Press, 2010.

White, Sam. "From Globalized Pig Breeds to Capitalist Pigs: A Study in Animal Cultures and Evolutionary History." *Environmental History* 16 (2011): 94–120.

B is also for . . .

Badger
Bat
Bullock
Buzzard

is for

CATTLE

THE CATTLE-DRUMMER.

The Baron of Beefferbrook *sings*:—
"OH, THE ROAST BEEF OF OLD CANADA,
AND OH, THE CANADIAN ROAST BEEF!"

C attle come from the family *Bovinae* and are colloquially
termed cows (female), bulls (uncastrated male), and ox (cas-
trated male). In Britain and across the empire, cattle were not
merely livestock: they were symbols of racial and imperial supremacy,
agents of empire, and sites of struggle at the same time. As domestic
animals, cattle represented the purported strength, vigor, and resil-
ience of the British populace. They symbolized the presumed cultural
superiority of Britain and the drive to reproduce it elsewhere. Cattle
featured prominently in the representational and racial politics of Britain, as so vividly evidenced in Edwin Landseer's famous 1867 painting, *Wild Cattle of Chillingham*. But they also carried a vital materiality,

....

"The Cattle Drummer." From *Punch,* August 22, 1922.

providing protein-rich food sources—meat and dairy—to an expanding British populace, both at home and abroad. Cattle figured as markers of agricultural progress, wealth, and status, as well as British law. Through the twinned imperial projects of agriculture and property acquisition, they extended Britain's imperial ambitions across land and sea. Given their symbolic and material import, cattle were the targets of anticolonial protest in many parts of the empire. Cattle thefts in North America and India, and cattle killings in South Africa, were forms of Indigenous struggle directed against colonial deterritorialization, including the pastoral imperial imaginaries in which colonial subjects were envisioned as hardy agriculturalists.

In the seventeenth and eighteenth centuries, cattle moved with sojourners and settlers to trading posts and frontier settlements, first as sources of food, and then as forms of property. In what is now Canada, the mainland United States, Hawai'i, and Australia, the transport of cattle was part of a much broader set of imperial aspirations aimed at transforming Indigenous lands into idyllic landscapes that would eventually be sites of permanent European resettlement. In the metropole and colonies, Britons constructed fences and enclosures to safeguard their livestock. Across the empire, the politics of protection engendered proprietary claims to cattle and to the lands upon which they grazed. Thus, as markers of agriculture and domesticity, cattle were important agents in British imperial expansion, particularly in the resettlement of the Dominions—Canada, Australia, and South Africa. They extended regimes of property and with it the authority and reach of British law. Cattle have a long history in conceptions of British legality. For example, the origin of imperial law has frequently been imagined through the figure of the plow. Etching lines in the soil and thereby distinguishing mine from thine, the plow instantiated new regimes of ownership. But the movements of the machine were impossible without the power of the ox. The imperial ambitions of law and agriculture came together in both physical and symbolic registers, reflecting British assertions of racial supremacy and imperial control.

Cattle were not indigenous to North America, Hawai'i, or Australia. Though they were brought to the far regions of Britain's empire through the movement of colonists and settlers, they became agents of colonization in their own right. The introduction of cattle allowed settlers new ways to dispossess Indigenous peoples from their ancestral lands, waterways, and natural resources, and to overwrite Indigenous claims to sovereignty and self-determination that remain ongoing sites of struggle today. In Hawai'i, cattle dramatically altered island environments by destroying local ecosystems. Cattle farming initiated processes of deforestation and introduced deadly diseases that carried serious implications for human and nonhuman ecologies. Cattle fed off plants that were vital to Indigenous life ways and also provided rationales for territorial displacement. But they also afforded new opportunities for Indigenous labor. In parts of North America and Australia, for example, Indigenous peoples were regularly recruited as cattle hands. What the politics of cattle tells us is that imperial struggles over land, labor, and resources were never human alone. They were deeply intertwined with the natural world, in ways that positioned animals as willful and disruptive agents of empire.

"The Cattle Drummer" was published in 1922 in the famous London magazine *Punch*. The first Baron Beaverbrook, William Maxwell Aitken, was a wealthy newspaper publisher who was born in Ontario. A millionaire by the age of thirty, he eventually moved to London, where he became a Conservative Member of British Parliament. *Punch* satirically named Aitken the Baron of Beeferbrook and pictured him singing a ballad—a play on the popular eighteenth-century tune "The Roast Beef of Old England." The original version, first performed in 1731, hailed beef as a staple in the Englishman's diet, a food source that produced national and racial supremacy: "When mighty Roast Beef was the Englishman's food, It ennobled our brains and enriched our blood. Our soldiers were brave and our courtiers were good. Oh! The Roast Beef of Old England, And Old English Roast Beef!" British sailors regularly performed this ballad on ships that traveled the high seas. Their audiences were first-class passengers traveling aboard British merchant ships, including the *Titanic*. In the ballad and beyond, the consumption of beef by British sailors, soldiers, courtiers, and ordinary men was viewed as a source of racial supremacy that supposedly gave Britons a biological, cultural, and military advantage over their European rivals, especially the French.

"The Roast Beef of Old England," as *Punch* suggests, eventually became "The Roast Beef of Old Canada." By the mid-nineteenth century, British cattle were subject to infectious diseases that resulted in a dramatic decline in beef supplies and national revenues. Britain's voracious cultural appetite for roast beef made it reliant on other parts of its empire. Between 1880 and 1910, Canada became a major producer of cattle, and Britain was its primary market. The transport of cattle from Montreal, along the St. Lawrence River and across the North

Atlantic to British ports of call—including Aberdeen, Dundee, and Thames—was thought to be a smooth journey, one that would ensure the arrival of healthy cattle ready for slaughter.

The transoceanic transport of cattle had legal, political, and ecological implications for settler colonial struggles over land. But it also extended Britannia's aspirations to rule the waves. The export of Canadian cattle to British ports is vividly portrayed in the imposing steamship represented in the *Punch* illustration. By the late nineteenth century, the conveyance of cattle across the North Atlantic engendered a series of heated discussions over the (in)humanity of cattle ships and the need to amend maritime laws and regulations that oversaw the marine transport of livestock. British Parliament passed a bill stating that cattle could be shipped only during certain months of the year, when the weather was mild and the sea was manageable. To maintain their health, livestock were to be kept on lower decks, in spaces that were well ventilated and sufficiently provisioned for their health and safety. Each animal was to have its own space, large enough so that it could stand up, lie down, and rest. The *Punch* illustration features a well-fed cow being led off the gangway from the ship's lower deck, presumably on its way to slaughter.

The transatlantic movements of cattle echo other histories of racial violence and imperial dominance. The nineteenth-century concerns regarding the wellbeing of cattle present a sharp, dramatic, and chilling contrast to the transatlantic slave trade. The humanitarian discourses that shaped the politics of cattle transport in the last decades of the nineteenth century may be read as originating in the rise of a liberal humanism that many have traced to the abolition of slavery. "Cattle" and "chattel" have a direct etymological connection. *Chatel* in Old French and *cattle* in Old North French convey the same meaning; both denote moveable property. Like cattle, African captives who were transported via ship and eventually sold as slaves were enumerated as cargo. The Atlantic passage was one in which the human/animal divide was both instantiated and undermined. Whereas captive Africans were transformed into commodities and then slaves, domestic animals were humanized through concerns about health and transport.

As cultural signifiers of British supremacy, it is perhaps unsurprising that cattle became a site of anticolonial struggle. In India, cattle were afforded cultural and religious meanings, including an exalted status among Hindus. The cow became an object of fierce contest that signaled the effects and vulnerabilities of British imperial rule (see Z IS FOR

ZEBU). In the eighteenth century, British colonists took their penchant for "The Roast Beef of Old England" with them to India. In 1760, Robert Clive, who served twice as the governor of Bengal, opened India's first slaughterhouse in Calcutta. His objectives were several: to disrupt the mythical status of the cow in the Hindu family, to unsettle the profitability of Indian agriculture, and to provide a steady supply of beef for Britons in India. However, British demands for beef came into direct conflict with the religious and cultural significance of cows among India's Hindu majority. In the famous rebellion of 1857, the cow featured prominently. Following rumors that rifle cartridges had been greased with pig and cow fat, Muslim and Hindu Sepoys rebelled against the British East India Company. From the 1880s onward, efforts to safeguard cows inspired a series of Indian anticolonial and nationalist initiatives, including cow protection societies and cow shelters known as *gaushalas*.

In India today, the cow has remained a site of political, legal, and racial contest that continues to reflect the longevity and durability of British imperialism. Following Indian independence, cow protection became a flashpoint of nationalist violence and a central organizing platform for the Hindu right. While the transportation and consumption of beef has been most closely associated with Muslims and has legitimized Islamophobia and other forms of violence, the Hindutva agendas of cow protection have more recently been directed at Dalits. Under the Hindu caste system, Dalits are responsible for the skinning, tanning, and interring of cows. Dalit men have been violently attacked by Hindu nationalists and advocates of cow protection societies who allege that they are responsible for cow killings. Religious and caste violence expressed through cow protection in contemporary India present one dramatic afterlife of British imperial rule. These instances demonstrate the ways in which cattle, once signs of British imperial and racial supremacy, are now the sites of virulent religious, racial, and nationalist violence.

Today, in the face of planetary climate change, cattle are no longer viewed as rich food sources, as they were under the British Empire. In many industrialized societies, cattle present one of the primary agents of deforestation, methane production, and carbon emissions. Environmentalists in western countries have strongly encouraged dietary changes—including a turn to alternative protein-rich foods such as insects and kangaroos—that might reduce beef consumption in order to save the planet. Contemporary ecological destruction wrought by cattle, we must remember, is an enduring effect of British imperial rule, one that is not often represented in discussions of climate change, the Anthropocene, or their historical causes.

Suggestions for Further Reading

Adock, Cassie, and Radhika Govindrajan. "Bovine Politics in South Asia: Rethinking Religion, Law, and Ethics." *South Asia: Journal of South Asian Studies* 42, 6 (2019): 1095–1107.

Ahuja, Neel. "On Phooka: Beef, Milk, and the Framing of Animal Cruelty in Late Colonial Bengal," in *Meat!*, edited by Sushmita Chatterjee and Banu Subramaniam. Durham, NC: Duke University Press, forthcoming.

Collingham, Lizzie. *Imperial Bodies: The Physical Experience of the Raj, 1800–1947*. Cambridge, UK: Polity, 2001.

Comaroff, John L., and Jean Comaroff. "Goodly Beasts, Beastly Goods: Cattle and Commodities in a South African Context." *American Ethnologist* 17, 2 (1990): 195–216.

Ferguson, James. "The Bovine Mystique: Power, Property, and Livestock in Rural Lesotho." *Man,* New Series, 20, 4 (1985): 647–74.

Fischer, John R. *Cattle Colonialism: An Environmental History of the Conquest of California and Hawai'i*. Chapel Hill: University of North Carolina Press, 2015.

Gilmartin, David. "Cattle, Crime and Colonialism: Property as Negotiation in North India." *Indian Economic and Social History Review* 40 (2003): 33–58.

Goldsmith, Oliver. *A History of the Earth and Animated Nature*. London, 1774.

Otter, Chris. "Civilized Slaughter: The Development of the British Abattoir, 1850–1910." *Food and History* 3, 2 (2006): 29–51.

Ritvo, Harriet. *The Animal Estate: The English and Other Creatures in Victorian England*. Cambridge, MA: Harvard University Press, 1989.

Velten, Hannah. *Cow*. London: Reaktion, 2007.

Vismann, Cornelia. "Starting from Scratch: Concepts of Order in No Man's Land." In *War, Violence, and the Modern Condition*, edited by Bernd Hüppauf, 46–64. New York: De Gruyter, 1997.

Wenzel, Jennifer. *Bulletproof: Afterlives of Anticolonial Prophecy in South Africa and Beyond*. Chicago: University of Chicago Press, 2009.

Yang, A. A. "Sacred Symbol and Sacred Space in Rural India: Community Mobilization in the 'Anti-Cow Killing' Riot of 1893." *Comparative Studies in Society and History* 22, 4 (1980): 576–96.

C is also for . . .

Camel
Caribou
Cat
Chameleon
Chimpanzee
Cobra

D

is for

DOG

For more than thirty thousand years, humans and dogs domesticated one another through the mutuality and immediacy of their needs. The relationship became significantly less egalitarian over the next several millennia, particularly in civilizational contexts where selective breeding commenced to create dogs physically tailored for war, hunting, herding, and even the sleeve or lap. With the rise of the British Empire, selective breeding assumed much greater political and economic importance as its productivity circulated through and gathered force from two imaginaries used to elaborate the international: the industrial *standard* and biological *race*, their synergy showing the degree to which empire and industry were inseparable. Standardization identified the uniformity of mechanically produced industrial goods with a purity reminiscent of race; race found in the standard new logical and practical means of hierarchically parsing, ordering, and organizing bodies and space. The machine's sheer material power and metering abilities carried the racial cruelties through which industrial *and* imperial-colonial life was recognized and made, including that of the canine.

· · · · · · · · · · · · · · · · · · ·

"Hark! Hark! The Dogs Do Bark" (London: Johnson and Riddle, 1914).

From the private collection of Panayotis N. Soucacos, MD, FACS.

How breed uniformity operated for imperial purposes can be seen in Cheang's vivid account of French and British troops ransacking China's imperial Summer Palace in 1860 during the Second Opium War and stealing at least five of the Empress Dowager Cixu's highly prized Pekingese dogs. British Captain John Hart Dunne purchased one specimen from French troops and gave it to Queen Victoria. She named it Looty and commissioned the well-known artist W. F. Keyl (1823–71) to paint its portrait, which was exhibited at the Royal Academy and hung in Windsor Castle. (Keyl's teacher, Sir Edwin Landseer, painted many of the queen's favorite animals, a few of which were gifts from other royalty.) Admiral John Hay gave two other Pekingese to the Duke of Gordon at Goodwood Castle. The last two were given to the Duchess of Richmond, who used them unsuccessfully to recreate what was (erroneously) thought to be a breed exclusive to the Chinese court. Eventually, elite English women would standardize the Pekingese, but only after securing additional specimens through military and (forced) diplomatic channels around the time of the Boxer Rebellion.

This confluence of uniformity and purity could have devastating consequences on indigenous dog populations in imperial contexts overseas. A senior medical officer accompanying British forces to Beijing during the Second Opium War recounted many instances of cruelty toward the dogs of rural Chinese, citing one case in which British officers amused themselves by skewering villagers' dogs with spears while on horseback. Similarly, in the 1890s, British forestry officials in the Eastern Cape of South Africa began poisoning local dogs that Africans had long used for hunting, rounding up livestock, and guarding their farms and homesteads. The officials did so, in part, to stop Indigenous men from hunting in the British forest-preserve system where colonial licensing restrictions and laws had already turned Native inhabitants and their dogs into poachers. While mass poisoning was ostensibly accomplished to aid preservation efforts, British sportsmen were allowed to use the forests to hunt "big game." Officialdom allowed deep licensing fee discounts to those who brought pedigree hunting dogs with them.

The mass poisoning of Eastern Cape dogs had widespread ecological effects. With the erosion of Indigenous hunting practices, large-animal populations grew. While welcomed by British sportsmen, these animals made African farm fields, livestock, and homes insecure. With less access to food sources and fewer means of socializing, many Africans entered the migrant labor system.

Colonial studies have made plain the imperial-racial utility of the pedigreed dog; the importance of pedigree to industry is less clear. For this we must look to the coalfields across the British Isles, which produced the most desirable energy source for industry and empire, and to the coal miners, who worked under exceptionally perilous circumstances. The most pressing and intimate of canine-human relationships—that between pitman and bull terrier—unfolded for mine workers. The bull terrier (referred to interchangeably here as the pit bull) helped make mining life tolerable, its fighting abilities honed and tested in the pit to enunciate a logos of social Darwinism decades before Darwin.

Pitmen probably bred the first bull terriers in the mid-1700s. They did so by crossbreeding a now-extinct version of the bulldog with various terrier kinds to create a companion with characteristics they themselves found necessary to survive: courage, tenacity, strength, and speed. Indeed, pitmen referred to themselves and their dogs as fighters and warriors. Pitmen exercised and trained the dogs and tested them regularly for "gameness" in the "pit." The earliest pits ranged from informal outdoor areas near or on colliery grounds to spaces inside or near the taverns where coal miners were paid, typically owned by mine managers. Here, two warriors of similar weight and size would be encouraged to "battle," the rules of competition varying regionally and over time. By the mid-nineteenth century, some pubs featured images of famous fighting dogs on their walls alongside images of famous bare-knuckle boxers, the two blood sports having emerged together. The athleticism and grittiness of the bull terrier helped make the violences of industry tolerable and therefore possible. The pit externalized the traumas that many pitmen faced. Hence, the coal pits could be reimagined as places of power rather than of defeat.

The blood sport traveled widely, spurred on by the proximity of mines to one another; the building of the extensive eighteenth-century canal system; historic levels of migration within the British Isles; the cultural prominence of pubs; the compactness of the pit bull body and pits; and the ease of setting up battles. Yet its expansion also came from how well the survivalist conditions and "gaming" of the pit helped make sense of the world. By the turn of the nineteenth century, British working-class men in other mining communities, provincial industrial towns, and large cities had likewise become aficionados—as were men of means, including aristocrats who had long dabbled in the sport. All found within the survivalist logos of the matches places from which to rally. Especially large battles were staged in commercial taverns dedicated to animal blood sports. London's famous Westminster Pit was built circa 1810 and catered to aristocrats and other elites, whose comparatively large wagers and (eventual) placement in the higher spectator tier of seating clarified their superior position. By the 1820s, even urban elites outside fighting circles had begun purchasing the dogs for what their fashionable fighting "look," exhibiting them by having them run after their carriages.

When Parliament banned animal blood sports in 1835, dogfighting went underground and expanded overseas. In the United States, Welsh colliers took the dogs to the coal mines of Pennsylvania and Ohio; the Cornish carried them to Colorado and the California Gold Rush. English and Irish immigrants brought them to the pubs of Boston and New York; sailors deposited them in the slave port of New Orleans. Pioneers brought them to help settle the frontier; southern U.S. plantation owners used them to catch runaway slaves. Similar human-dog migrations ensued to the colonies: British miners took the dogs with them to Nova Scotia, Australia, and South Africa; British soldiers brought them to India and Pakistan; sailors carried them to and from port cities worldwide. The purview of the pitted dog accordingly expanded to entertain the isolating anxieties and terrors of empire-building, and the class-striated masculinity peculiar to this compact grew to assume direct racial force.

The 1835 Parliamentary ban did effect some changes, however. Most notably, it put the large commercial taverns out of the dogfighting business. Some publicans consequently looked to profit from a new canine craze unfolding among the working class: the "toy breed," originally an aristocratic preserve that had recently been taken up by the bourgeoisie. The pugilist-publican Charles Aistrop (whose father once owned the Westminster Pit) helped establish England's first Toy Dog Club sometime in the 1830s, well before British forces stole the Pekingese from the Summer Palace. In 1852, he went on to sponsor the first-ever Fancy Dog Show in his St. Giles Street pub, for which he charged a gate fee. This was a good eight years before provincial aristocratic elites and industrialists in Newcastle-on-Tyne staged their own show, featuring aristocratic hunting dogs and based on poultry and livestock exhibition precedents. By 1867, more than fifty pubs across London's poorer districts were hosting gated toy dog shows, presumably spurred on by the recent imperial import of the Pekingese. These myriad tavern events made plain the great interest that the working-class poor had in understanding and articulating the value of racial uniformity, even if the vernacular scale and commonness of the pubs did not translate into spectacle.

The elite 1859 Newcastle-on-Tyne show, by contrast, did. Within a year, similarly patronized and increasingly well-funded events open to all sorts of pedigrees were unfolding in cities and towns across Britain. Aspiring members of the middle class flocked to these shows, finding in the decorum, exclusive location, and accessibility a world in which industrial-imperial violences were rarefied and forcibly, aesthetically, silenced. The dog fancy of old (dogfighting) thus migrated away from the pit, bareknuckle boxing, and pub and toward the highly vested bourgeois show bench and ring. Traces of the pit nevertheless remained, sedimented into the show ring's language of battles, champions, and championships and in the standardized remaking of a docile, show-worthy pit bull.

Ironically, this remaking took place in Birmingham, a great imperial dogfighting hub and center of industry and innovation. Here, dogmen (a euphemism for those invested in dogfighting) had refused to abide by the 1835 parliamentary decree. That is, until 1839, when members of the newly minted Metropolitan Police Force were sent to shut down the city's public dogfighting pit and jail offenders. As in other areas, the shutdown was not about improving human or dog conditions but about rising bourgeois sensibilities, as James Hinks's selective breeding of the bull terrier would make plain.

Hinks and his family had left Ireland for Birmingham in 1851, on the heels of the English-induced Great Famine. At first, Hinks labored in one of the many brass foundries for which the city had become famous. He soon married, became a registered trader and poultry dealer, and started breeding birds, rabbits, and dogs, which may explain how he came to know the future owner of Crufts. As in London decades earlier, the fighting look of the bull terrier had become popular. Hinks set out to create a commercially uniform variety which, to be successful, would have to pass muster in the show ring. In time, Hinks produced several iterations of an all-white and docile dog that he exhibited at dozens of shows across Britain with great success, including the 1864 show at London's prestigious Cremorne Gardens. Fighting dogmen scorned his efforts, refusing to acknowledge the value of a dog that only looked like it could fight.

The 1863 Cremorne Gardens show was the earliest and grandest dog event ever—a week-long extravaganza on former aristocratic grounds.

One thousand dogs were entered, and over one hundred thousand persons attended, including the Prince and Princess of Wales, who exhibited breeds from India, Russia, and Newfoundland. Their royalty and the exoticized provenance of the breeds they presented fed into a racially principled imaginary of empire. Two months later, dog enthusiasts in France staged that nation's first dog show. The Exposition universelle des races canines was held in the Jardin zoologique d'acclimatation outside Paris, with Prince Napoleon exhibiting his foxhounds. Such canine-inflected racial geographies of empire would assume cartographic proportions by the end of empire, through maps satirically depicting European imperial powers as purebred dogs. One example is "Hark! Hark! The Dogs Do Bark!," published in 1914. The map takes its title from an English nursery rhyme with political origins and uses that may date back to the eleventh century. Each major European imperial power figures as a distinct pedigree of canine-men, except for Austria, which the caption deems a mongrel. Turkey, by contrast, is represented by the "dog of Constantinople," said to be an offal-eating cur. Thus, the distinctions of pedigree first made in imperial Britain allowed the dog to be used as a racialized geopolitical device.

The most extreme biological lengths (inbreeding and culling) taken to ensure the uniformity of a particular racial look did not become de rigueur, however, until the Kennel Club (KC) formed in 1873 in response to accusations of show-ring cheating. Some exhibitors and dog merchants had started cosmetically altering a nonstandard dog's appearance to make it look like a pedigree. Kennel Club founders consequently focused on identifying and registering an originary pair for each show breed and measuring and recording the pair's physiognomic characteristics in detail. These records became the basis of each breed's *conformation* standard, an imaginary unit of racial fixity by which progeny found to be lacking could justifiably be culled. Henceforth, only conformational progeny would be allowed into the ring, the constitutional violence of this fact pointing to the *reproductive* anxieties underpinning all imperial-industrial taxonomic and standard-making endeavors. The first KC-sponsored show took place in 1873 in London's Crystal Palace and boasted 975 entrants. The event legitimated the KC as the preeminent authority on canine standards in Britain and rationalized the business of show dogs and dog shows.

The dog's exceptional potential for phenotypical variation, along with its loyalty and companionate graces, ironically advanced the bodily and cartographic fixing of race across industry and empire.

Even so, the bull terrier was the first dog to be bred for the broadest of imperial-industrial purposes. Its tenacity and fighting skills allowed early miners to stage and circumscribe the disciplinary violences of their own exploitation and inspired a survivalist manhood with devastating raced and gendered consequences domestically and overseas. The show dog and dog show, by contrast, rendered the reproductive violences of industry and empire aesthetic. This gave women entry and provided all social classes with means for positioning and fashioning themselves in an empire metered by racialized standard-making.

With the rise of finance capitalism, pitted dogfighting has expanded greatly into new survivalist reaches of masculinity and the racialized poor. By contrast, the violence of inbreeding and culling that made the show dog and dog show possible is now imploding upon itself, as genetic defects proliferate and the biology of the dog speaks its own truth to power.

Suggestions for Further Reading

Brown, Laura. *Homeless Dogs and Melancholy Apes: Humans and Other Animals in the Modern Literary Imagination*. Ithaca, NY: Cornell University Press, 2017.

Cheang, Sarah. "Women, Pets, and Imperialism: The British Pekingese Dog and Nostalgia for Old China. *Journal of British Studies* 45 (2006): 359–87.

Germonpre, Mietje, Martina Laznickova Galetova, Robert J. Losey, Jannikke Raikkonen, Mikhail V. Sablin. "Large Canids at the Gravettian Predmostí Site, the Czech Republic: The Mandible." *Quarternary International* 359 (2015): 261–79.

Howell, Philip. *At Home and Astray: The Domestic Dog in Victorian Britain*. Charlottesville: University of Virginia Press, 2015.

Huff, Cynthia. "Victorian Exhibitionism and Eugenics: The Case of Francis Galton and the 1899 Crystal Palace Dog Show." *Victorian Review* 28, 2 (2002): 1–20.

Jaquet, Edward Williams. *The Kennel Club: A History and Record of its Work*. London: The Kennel Gazette, 1905.

Lane, Charles H. *Dog Shows and Doggy People*. London: Hutchison and Co., 1902.

Nast, Heidi J. "For the Love of Life: Coal Mining and Pit Bull Fighting in 19th Century Great Britain." In *Historical Animal Geographies*, edited by Stephanie Rutherford and Sharon Wilcox, 275–93. London: Routledge, 2018.

Rappaport, Helen. *Queen Victoria: A Biographical Companion*. Oxford, UK: ABC-CLIO, 2003.

Rennie, David Field. *The British Arms in North China and Japan: Peking 1860; Kagosima 1862*. London: Murray, 1864.

Ritvo, Harriet. "Pride and Pedigree: The Evolution of the Victorian Dog Fancy." *Victorian Studies* 29, 2 (1986): 227–53.

Thomas, Richard. "Perceptions versus Reality: Changing Attitudes towards Pets in Medieval and Post-Medieval England." In *Just Skin and Bones? New Perspectives on Human-Animal Relations in the Historic Past*, edited by Aleksander Pluskowski, 95–105. Oxford, UK: Archaeopress, 2005.

Tropp, Jacob. "Dogs, Poison and the Meaning of Colonial Intervention in the Transkei, South Africa." *Journal of African History* 43, 2 (2002): 451–72.

Waters, B. "The Pariah Dogs of Constantinople Turkey." *World Wide Magazine*, November 1898, 209–13.

D is also for . . .

Deer
Dhole
Dingo
Dolphin
Duck

is for

ELEPHANT

The chaotic scene is an elephant steeplechase, an improbable race held in Rangoon in 1858. The famous Shwedagon Pagoda is visible in the background. According to the newspaper report that accompanied the illustration, the British officers stationed at the local garrison had organized the event as part of their celebrations marking Queen Victoria's birthday. They dressed as jockeys and raced the elephants—although all *they* actually did was sit on their animals' backs while the creatures were "steered" by mahouts. This reliance on preexisting elephant expertise was typical; all British uses of elephants relied upon the skills and knowledge of colonized people. The local population placed bets on the elephant they thought would win. According to the correspondent, the excitement of gambling meant that the artist "allowed his pencil to be carried away, a little, by his feelings when he was portraying them." On the right-hand side of the picture is a ditch—three feet deep, seven feet long—that was used as the third

. . . .

"Elephant Steeplechase at Rangoon, Burma." From *Illustrated London News*, September 25, 1858. Used by permission of Getty Images, object number: PPP30161805.

jump. None of the elephants jumped it. Predictably, they clambered in and out of it, the author noted with mirth, "like elephants!"

Although bizarre, the image captures two routine ways that elephants were used by the British Empire: as instruments and as ornaments. In this particular case, they were both. As the property of the military, they were instruments of warfare. The year before this unlikely elephantine obstacle course was concocted, the East India Company had attempted to acquire as many elephants as it could from the newly colonized territory of Lower Burma to help with the suppression of the Indian Rebellion, which had swept through northern India. By the end of the century, their instrumental utility had shifted from primarily military to commercial use. Across the Indian subcontinent, British timber firms acquired large herds, in some cases several thousand elephants, to help with logging. In this semicaptive state, they were deployed to fell timber, contributing to deforestation and the destruction of their own habitats.

They were also used as ornaments. In Rangoon, they were part of the entertainments arranged to mark an imperial celebration. As British imperialism in the subcontinent moved out of the hands of the Company and into direct government oversight from London in the nineteenth century, no durbar or formal state procession would have been complete without a parade of nobles and officials being carried on the backs of elephants. More widely, both African and Asian elephants were captured and displayed across Britain in the numerous traveling menageries and zoos of the nineteenth and twentieth centuries. Even less fortunate than these captive beasts were the animals shot by big-game hunters who turned their carcasses into macabre souvenirs. Beyond the physical creature, the image and imagery of elephants became ubiquitous in imperial Britain, in iconography, advertising, and literature. In children's alphabet books, representation of the letter "E" went from elder tree to "elephant" over the course of the nineteenth century. However, in deploying elephants as instruments and ornaments, the colonial authorities did not always have things their own way.

At its height, the empire included territories in which all three species of elephant resided. In South and Southeast Asia, the British encountered *Elephas maximus*, or the Asian elephant. Trade relations between the Company and South Asian polities contributed greatly to early modern scientific knowledge about this species. In East and Southern Africa, the British Empire encroached on the habitats of the two species of African Elephant: *Loxodonta africana*, the bush elephant;

and *Loxodonta cyclotis*, the forest elephant. The African species can be distinguished from their distant relatives on the other side of the Indian Ocean by their greater size, larger ears, wrinkly skin, and two finger-like tips on the end of their trunk, as opposed to one. African forest elephants have rounder ears and narrower tusks than bush elephants; only recently were the two species found to be distinct. In both Asia and Africa, the history of imperialism had profound implications for elephant populations.

Precolonial polities in East Africa had been involved in hunting elephants for the long-distance trade in ivory for centuries prior to European conquest. This trade expanded into the nineteenth century with growing demand for luxury goods in Europe, as well as the shifting locus of the caravan trade between the interior and the coast. This was also a time when predations on the elephant population were added to by that eminent imperial archetype, the big-game hunter. These so-called sportsmen (and they were predominantly, although not exclusively, men) came to be seen as the legitimate killers of elephants. Colonial game regulations and subsequent wildlife conservation laws distinguished between "white hunters" and "Black poachers." Legislation that protected the animals in sanctuaries in Kenya and South Africa, popular destinations for hunting, were often funded by licensed hunting. The rules governing who was and was not permitted to kill an elephant were bound up with racial and class privilege. As a result, the colonial period coincided with dramatic falls in the numbers of surviving elephants in the continent.

Dead African elephants were not only turned into ornaments through the appropriation of their tusks for ivory. The remains of elephants were occasionally turned into ghoulish furniture, such as stools made out of their feet. Their bodies were butchered and they were re-animated through taxidermy for display in museums across the world. Live elephants, too, became commodities that circulated around the globe. Their capture would invariably involve the deaths of their kin. These were traumatic experiences for elephants that would leave both physical and mental scars. In Europe and America, their fate lay in the overlapping realms of entertainment and science in traveling menageries, zoos, and circuses. Some became celebrities. The African bush elephant, Jumbo, became a firm favorite in Victorian Britain. Born in Sudan in roughly 1860, he was captured after hunters killed his mother. He traveled across North Africa and the Mediterranean and spent time in Germany and France before arriving in the London Zoological Gardens in 1865. He attracted huge crowds, and visitors would bring him iced buns and other sugary treats. When the zoo decided to sell him to the now-notorious American showman P. T. Barnum, there was widespread upset—much of it bound up with a sense of injured national pride. As the public connection with Jumbo showed, elephants came to be recognized to be individuals with their own internal worlds, worthy of recognition and sympathy.

In addition to making African elephants into ornaments, there were attempts to turn them into instruments that could be deployed for imperial ends. Some efforts were made to train African elephants for work, but the use of captive elephants for work in Africa did not become widespread—although they continue to be used to transport people on safaris. Nevertheless, through their own willful labors, these giants influence the landscapes and environments of human societies. They are "ecosystem engineers" whose migrations create pathways through difficult terrain, whose diets distribute seeds, and who seek out and make available sources of water. The history of African elephants' interactions with humans has involved conflict—in many ways exacerbated by empire—but also coexistence and cohabitation, although finding an equilibrium among the needs of the three species remains an ongoing problem.

The widespread semidomestication of Asian elephants led to their greater exploitation by imperial authorities. The skills involved in capturing, training and driving an elephant had long been central to southern Asian kingship. The war elephant was a pivotal part of an early modern army in the region. Their military prominence may help to explain why the species survived in this part of the continent when they became extinct in most of China during the same time period. British imperialism built on these long-standing human-elephant relationships and expanded them. As we have seen, elephants were enlisted into the Indian Army. While their strategic importance and role diminished during the nineteenth century, as they went from being direct combatants to providing logistical assistance as transportation, they did not disappear from theatres of conflict. In the dramatic British retreat from Burma in the face of Japanese conquests in 1942, elephants helped carry refugees across the treacherous mountain border with India. They later contributed just as much to the eventual reoccupation.

As their military use declined, their industrial use grew. They were found to be especially well suited to logging. From the late nineteenth century, demand for timber soared, and the numbers of working elephants rose too, tipping the balance of the population from wild to semi-captive. They helped transport human labor to forests. Their strength was vital in felling the trees. Their stamina allowed them to drag the trunks to waterways, down which the logs would travel. If the rivers became jammed, an elephant could swim to dislodge the blockage. In urban sawmills, their dexterity was advantageous when it came to moving and maneuvering the timber. Their widely acknowledged utility, coupled with fears about their falling numbers—exacerbated by hunting—led to legislative measures to protect them, which were introduced and expanded across British India from 1879.

Whether used as instruments or ornaments, elephants were not easily coopted for imperial ends. Capturing elephants from the wild—whichever method was used—was a traumatic and violent experience. Once captured, the process of "breaking" and training them could be brutal. At its best, maintaining them in subservience meant a life of stressful semicaptivity. But they were not passive or docile. Elephants are powerful, intelligent creatures, and they showed their justified displeasure frequently. Asian elephant-drivers and the laborers who worked alongside these giant creatures usually bore the brunt of their anger. Some working elephants went rogue, escaped, and became a menace to their former captors. Wild elephants would pilfer human crops and cause trouble for the herds of working elephants. In some unfortunate incidents, they would be involved in collisions that derailed trains, the consequence of newly laid railways crossing across their territories. These episodes were reported as clashes between modernity and tradition, overlooking the essential labor done by elephants in extracting, transporting, and laying the timber sleepers upon which the trains themselves ran.

British colonizers may have harnessed elephant power, but it was always a fragile and incomplete authority that was held over them. Unable to understand how their circumstances were being increasingly shaped by global capitalism and imperial cultures, elephants nonetheless adapted, resisted, and survived their encounter with the empire, albeit becoming endangered species in the process. Few texts captured the ambivalence of the elephant's entanglement with British imperialism as well as George Orwell's famous anti-imperial essay "Shooting an Elephant." Orwell exposed the psychological fragility of white colonial officials performing the role of tyrant by retelling his own experiences dealing with a working elephant in Burma. The elephant had broken free of its shackles and killed an Indian laborer in an outburst of musth (aggressive behavior). Orwell did not want to kill the elephant; he felt sympathy for the creature, and it was a useful, valuable beast. But he had to shoot the animal so as to demonstrate that he was in charge.

Suggestions for Further Reading

Amato, Sarah. "The White Elephant in London: An Episode of Trickery, Racism and Advertising." *Journal of Social History* 43, 1 (2009): 31–66.

Cowie, Helen. *Exhibiting Animals in Nineteenth-Century Britain: Empathy, Education, Entertainment*. Basingstoke, UK: Palgrave Macmillan, 2014.

Heintzman, Alix. "E is for Elephant: Jungle Animals in Late Nineteenth-Century Picture Books." *Environmental History* 19, 3 (2014): 553–63.

Nance, Susan. *Entertaining Elephants: Animal Agency and the Business of the American Circus*. Baltimore, MD: Johns Hopkins University Press, 2013.

Nance, Susan. *Animal Modernity: Jumbo the Elephant and the Human Dilemma*. Basingstoke, UK: Palgrave Macmillan, 2015.

Orwell, George. *Shooting an Elephant*. London: Penguin, 2009.

Saha, Jonathan. "Colonizing Elephants: Animal Agency, Undead Capital and Imperial Science in British Burma." *BJHS Themes* 2 (2017): 169–89.

Sivasundaram, Sujit. "Trading Knowledge: The East India Company's Elephants in India and Britain." *Historical Journal* 48, 1 (2005): 27–63.

Steinhart, Edward I. *Black Poachers, White Hunters: A Social History of Hunting in Colonial Kenya*. Oxford, UK: Currey, 2006.

Trautmann, Thomas R. *Elephants and Kings: An Environmental History*. Chicago: University of Chicago Press, 2015.

E is also for . . .

Eagle

Earwig

Emu

Eastern Gorilla

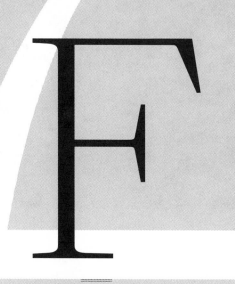

F

is for

FOX

F ew animals loom as large in the British imagination as the fox. A symbol of stealth and the tenacity of the natural world, the fox has been the favorite quarry of the nation's hunters for two hundred years. Although foxhunting, with its highly formalized dress, etiquette, and vocabulary, is a well-known symbol of "traditional" British culture, it is not an ancient sport. Chasing foxes on horseback with hounds was an eighteenth-century invention that reached its high point during the Victorian era—coincident with the rise of the British Empire. Indeed, as their overseas empire grew, the British took this strange sport with them around the globe, regardless of its dire impact on the local environment or local populations.

Since ancient times, foxes have symbolized cunning, duplicity, and theft. In *Aesop's Fables*, foxes foil (outfox) bigger and stronger animals;

....

"A Fox Hunt Interrupted by a Crowd of Peasants," Ireland. From *L'Illustrazione Italiana*, January 15, 1882. Used by permission of Getty Images, object number: 933479362.

in the Bible, they are "the little foxes that spoil the vines." The British seldom attributed vulpine (foxlike) qualities to themselves, preferring to see their enemies (French) or colonized people (Irish, Indians) as foxy—sly and conniving. For instance, in his 1877 *History of India*, Sir Henry Elliot denounces the "fox-like habits" of Hindu princes. The radical politician Charles James Fox, who sympathized with the American revolutionaries, was often depicted in cartoons as his animal namesake by his conservative, pro-empire detractors.

Nowhere was the English aversion to the fox underscored so dramatically as in the fox hunt, a highly ritualized upper-class pastime. The hard-riding, foxhunting squire came to embody the aggressive values of the British ruling class—the very men who had built the empire. If, as the Duke of Wellington famously claimed, the Battle of Waterloo was won on the playing fields of Eton, then the British Empire itself was the natural outcome of foxhunting. In 1826, the writer John Cook argued that foxhunting developed brave, hardy men, and that without it, "you would have nothing but an effeminate race," incapable of defending the empire. In 1860, R. H. W. Dunlop agreed that hunting was essential in developing the "manly qualities" necessary for imperialism. He insisted that the "Anglo-Saxons are the only true sportsmen in the world," and that the hunt endowed them with "energy of mind and body . . . which they carry with them wherever they wander." Though foxhunting was praised as the ideal training for an imperial people, its actual practice throughout the empire was fraught with difficulties.

In the wider empire, as in Britain, foxhunting exacerbated class conflict between the landowning elite and their tenants. In England, aristocrats had long maintained preserves of game animals that fed on their neighbors' crops and killed their livestock. In a colonial setting, British hunting privileges aggravated ethnic and racial inequalities as well as class divisions. As historian John Mackenzie emphasizes, the sporting needs of British hunters turned vermin into a protected species, to the consternation of subject peoples.

Closest to home, in Ireland, foxhunting amplified tensions between "Native" Irish Catholic peasants and an Anglo-Protestant colonial elite. British landowners maintained artificially high fox populations for their hunting pleasure. This angered Irish tenant farmers, who viewed foxes as pests that preyed upon their chickens and geese. If farmers destroyed foxes themselves, they could be prosecuted for poaching, a capital crime until 1831. During fox hunts, horses and hounds tore across open fields and gardens, trampling crops in their path—a potent symbol of British imperialism and aristocratic privilege. The Irish wit Oscar Wilde sarcastically described the foxhunting Englishman as "the unspeakable in pursuit of the uneatable." Irish patriots later opposed foxhunting on nationalist grounds, poisoning foxes and organizing anti-hunting mobs to disrupt hunts. A print from 1882 shows a group of Irish peasants confronting the local foxhunting elite. During the 1880s, the Irish Land League sponsored "people's hunts," in which Irish tenant farmers openly poached game like foxes, hares, and pheasants.

In other parts of the empire, foxhunting became a popular sport for colonial officials, military officers, and anyone wanting to assert a British identity or uphold British values. As early as the 1790s, British nabobs in India began breeding foxhounds. Several colonial governors and viceroys presided over fox hunts as the Master of Hounds. This office was considered a great honor. But it was far from a sinecure: at least two Canadian governors died while foxhunting, one from a riding accident, the other after being bitten by a fox. Some Australians praised the invigorating effect of foxhunting on the colony's youth as a healthier alternative to lounging in pubs and cafes. The hunt became yet another way for colonists to perform Britishness, like wearing tweed, drinking tea, or celebrating Queen Victoria's birthday. To carry out the proud traditions of the English fox hunt in distant lands bolstered one's standing in the colonial community and demonstrated one's right to rule over less civilized peoples.

Foxhunting also allowed colonial participants to play at being landed gentry. Hunters in distant outposts in Australia, Canada, and India included a wider assortment of social classes than in England, where the sport was decidedly aristocratic. In India whiteness conferred elite status, and therefore the right to participate in the hunt as gentlemen. As one anonymous Anglo-Indian noted in verse, the empire afforded ordinary Britons unique hunting opportunities:

If you don't expect a treasure and go in for moderate measure,
You can pick up sport and leisure which at Home you cannot get.

Not everyone became rich in India, but at least they could hunt like a lord.

Replicating the English fox hunt in a wide variety of colonial landscapes was no easy matter, but the determination to do so was thought to exemplify the British "bulldog spirit." In 1842, the *Asiatic Journal and*

Monthly Register for British India lovingly narrated the struggle of some British soldiers stationed near Madras to organize a foxhunting club. While the club had to make do with chasing jackals in fox-free India, the men drew the line at using Indian dogs. The native greyhounds were excellent hunters but didn't bray like English beagles, and the soldiers grew nostalgic for that "spirit-stirring music" of the hunt. The men imported six English foxhounds at considerable expense. They also devised a fancy club uniform of "green riding coat, with fox button, buff waistcoat and white-cord breeches." For these soldiers, the obsession with replicating the proper form of an English hunt was not trivial. Their attention to detail was another way to draw distinctions between rulers and ruled. Unlike the slipshod "Native," the British ruling class understood the true spirit of the hunt.

The imperial export of foxhunting also had ecological implications, most disastrously in Australia. In 1845,the European red fox was introduced into the continent merely for hunting. Previously, Australian hunt clubs had chased dingoes and kangaroos, but traditionalists longed for English foxes (see J IS FOR JACKAL). Some Australians denounced the introduction of foxes as an "insane delusion" of hunting enthusiasts, but they were primarily concerned with potential threats to domestic lambs and poultry. These fears proved correct. By the 1880s, foxes had become such a menace to livestock that the state of Victoria offered a bounty for each fox killed, and the state of South Australia passed a Fox Destruction Act. At the time, Australians expressed less concern for foxes' decimation of native fauna; but by the 1890s, imported foxes had seriously eroded several indigenous species of birds (stone plovers, mallee fowl, lyre-birds) and small mammals (kangaroo rats, wallabies, bandicoots). In other colonies, foxes were overprotected. The animals that preyed on them, like badgers, wolverines, and coyotes, were trapped or poisoned, further upsetting local ecosystems.

As the British Empire receded in the decades following World War II, so too did enthusiasm for foxhunting. Earlier centuries had seen the natural world (and the fox) as something wild and dangerous that needed to be subdued, but contemporary society was more inclined to cherish and protect what little remained of the countryside. Animal rights activists condemned foxhunting as a cruel blood sport; Labour Party politicians denounced it as a grotesque survival of "tally-ho" aristocratic privilege. The hunt was severely restricted in 2004, despite Conservative attempts to depict it as a healthy recreation of country people and an "authentic fragment" of Ye Olde England.

In Britain, the fox has had the last word. No longer pursued by horse and hound but by creeping suburbanization, foxes have colonized British cities, especially London. They have migrated into the capital in the thousands, along railway lines and canals, taking up residence in public parks and domestic gardens. No longer raiding the farmer's henhouse, urban foxes feast on the city's abundant garbage and its vast populations of rats, squirrels, and pigeons, with an occasional house pet to vary their diet.

Ironically, despite Britain's ban on blood sports, foxhunting lives on in some former British colonies, like Ireland and Canada, where it is celebrated as a "traditional" rural pastime. Romanticized depictions of the hunt also endure in popular television series like *Downton Abbey*, symbolizing a lost world of manor houses and gracious country living. Rose-colored views of the fox hunt are bound up with nostalgia for the Empire and Britain's lost global authority.

Suggestions for Further Reading

Abbot, Ian. "The Importation, Release, Establishment, Spread, and Early Impact on Prey Animals of the Red Fox *Volpes volpes* in Victoria and Adjoining parts of South-Eastern Australia." *Australian Zoologist* 35, 3 (2011): 463–533.

Bennett, Scott. "*Shikar* and the Raj." *South Asia* 7 (1984): 72–88.

Curtis, L. P. "Stopping the Hunt." In *Nationalism and Popular Protest in Ireland*, edited by C. H. E. Philpin, 349–402. Cambridge, UK: Cambridge University Press, 1987.

Howe, James. "Fox Hunting as Ritual." *American Ethnologist* 8 (1981): 278–300.

Itzkowitz, David C. *Peculiar Privilege: A Social History of English Fox-hunting, 1753–1885*. Brighton, UK: Harvester, 1977.

Jones, Lucy. *Foxes Unearthed: A Story of Love and Loathing in Modern Britain*. London: Elliott and Thompson, 2017.

Kirk-Greene, Anthony. "Badge of Office?: Sport and His Excellency in the British Empire." *International Journal of the History of Sport* 6 (1989) 218–41.

May, Allyson. *The Fox-Hunting Controversy, 1781–2004: Class and Cruelty*. Farnham, UK: Ashgate, 2013.

Mukherjee, Pablo. "Nimrods: Hunting, Authority, Identity." *Modern Language Review* 100, 4 (2005): 923–39.

Newell, Venetia. "The Unspeakable in Pursuit of the Uneatable: Some Comments on Fox-Hunting." *Folklore* 94 (1983): 86–90.

F is also for . . .

Flamingo
Fire ant
Frog

is for

GIRAFFE

The GIRAFFES with the ARABS who brought them over to this Country ZOOLOGICAL GARDENS, Regent's Park

In 1836, the Zoological Society of London's five-year effort to acquire giraffes for its collection was finally nearing fruition. British endeavors to capture and ship giraffes had failed; but a French trader named George Thibaut, working in concert with several Sudanese men, had captured four giraffes—one female and three males—and transported them as far as Malta. But just as the ZSL was on the brink of success, news came of another shipment of giraffes en route to the Surrey Zoological Gardens. The cachet of offering the first publicly viewable giraffes in Britain was such that the ZSL agreed to pay an additional £2000—nearly £100,000 in today's money—for faster transport that could outrace the Surrey Zoo's giraffes.

Remarkably, this was a wise decision. In his history of the London Zoo, Takashi Ito reports that over four thousand people visited the zoo the first Sunday after the giraffe exhibit opened. A news account at the time stated that weekly ticket sales averaged £600 for several months afterwards. No doubt the Surrey Zoo also saw increased atten-

....

"Three [*sic*] Giraffes Surrounded by Men in Arabic Costume." Zoological Society of London. Colored lithograph by G. Scharf, 1836. Source: Wellcome Collection, CC BY 4.0, https://wellcomecollection.org/works/tz9um9ps.

dance when their giraffes arrived six weeks later, but it was the ZSL's giraffes and Thibaut's expedition that became the subject of popular attention.

When the ZSL decided to hire the faster steamer, they were not concerned simply with ticket sales; indeed, those learned gentlemen would have disdained such a suggestion. They wanted the giraffes because the still little-known animals would add to the prestige of their institution and to British science more generally, even though these would not be the first giraffe to grace the shores of Britain. Nine years earlier, a giraffe had been given as a diplomatic gift to King George IV by the Ottoman governor-general of Egypt, Mehmed Ali Pasha. Mehmed Ali had his own expansionist goals and sent giraffes to the monarchs of Britain, France, and Austria as part of an effort to secure their goodwill toward his imperial ambitions. In each country, the giraffes sparked a craze, inspiring fashions, foods, and objet d'art. The craze was more muted in England, however: King George IV kept his giraffe at Windsor, and comparatively few people saw it before it died two years later. The Austrian giraffe also died quickly. The French, on the other hand, had installed their giraffe in the Jardin des Plantes in Paris, where it remained on public display until its death in 1840.

By the early 1800s, the scientific quest for knowledge that dated back to the Enlightenment had become nationalist in tone, and the comparative success of the French giraffe rankled in Britain. Bringing four healthy giraffes to London enabled British naturalists to tip the balance in their favor. It was equally important to the nascent ZSL, with its royal charter and status as a national institution, that they not be bested by the commercial Surrey Zoo founded by Edward Cross, an animal importer and former manager of King George IV's menagerie. Collecting and strategically displaying animals and even plants was a key component of building one's scientific reputation during this era. In that context, the money invested by the ZSL simply to be the first British zoo to display giraffes was well spent.

It was simple curiosity, though, that drew many to the exhibit. Giraffes are the tallest land animals, and they were unlike anything most Britons had ever seen. Just fifty years previously, British naturalists had still doubted whether such an animal was real or not. The descriptions they had of a creature shaped like a camel, but with spots like a leopard, certainly sounded more suited to legend than life. The ZSL's new giraffes, who managed to be at once graceful and awkward, elegant and gangly, did not disappoint.

The mystique surrounding the giraffes was also heightened by the presence of the giraffes' three Sudanese keepers, named Cabas, Omar, and Abdalah. The expedition leader, George Thibaut, was also on hand during the opening days. He obligingly contributed to the mise-en-scène by dressing in the traditional garb of an Ottoman Turk—the Ottoman Empire still having nominal control over Egypt, which governed the Sudan. Together, the giraffes and four men were featured in a fashionable print, which was then replicated in an extensive line of pottery. Such merchandise took the imagery of this display beyond the London zoo's walls and into people's homes throughout the kingdom.

From the perspective of contemporaries, however, there was nothing inherently imperialist about the image of four giraffes and their keepers. It was a Frenchman working through international and scientific networks who had brought them to London. The British Empire had no colonial ambitions in the Sudan, and would not for nearly fifty more years. Many people probably never thought explicitly of the empire when viewing the giraffes or one of the many images created of them. Yet British scientists' desire to procure the giraffes had gained impetus from Britain's imperial rivalry with France. The decision to showcase Thibaut, Cabas, Omar, and Abdalah with the giraffes reflected—and in its own way contributed to—the notions of difference and superiority that justified Britain's imperial expansion in the nineteenth century.

The portrayal of the Sudanese keepers was a far cry from the overtly racist "human zoo" exhibits of the late 1800s or of Saartjie Baartman, the so-called Hottentot Venus, who was displayed nearly naked and sometimes caged for the titillation of audiences in Britain and France in the 1810s. The Sudanese keepers were not themselves the exhibit, and their formal clothing marked them as exotic foreigners rather than as savages or specimens. Yet they were still part of the attraction. By creating a space for Cabas, Abdalah, and Omar to relax within the animal enclosure, the ZSL effectively put them on display alongside their animal charges, much to the men's reported annoyance.

The attention directed at the Sudanese keepers shows that the public fascination with the giraffes stemmed in part from an interest in their homeland. It was no coincidence that George IV's and the French giraffes had also been painted with their Egyptian and Sudanese keepers. In each case, people saw the caretakers not as expert attendants but as picturesque Natives. Like the subjects of human zoos, they became objects for study and amusement. Visitors could stare, point, and comment at will as they gazed at men whom they saw as both exotic and culturally backward. George Thibaut obligingly made a spectacle of himself as well; but in the mid-century, Britons celebrated Western men who had ostensibly mastered other languages and cultures to the extent that they could pass undetected in foreign lands. Thus, his position as the expedition leader and even his showy attire further suggested the Sudanese men's subservient position. Intentionally or not, the pottery line that replicated George Scharf's popular lithograph of the group emphasized this reading by omitting Cabas and Omar, leaving just Abdalah, kneeling before Thibaut.

These images immortalized the hierarchical and romanticized vision of the giraffes' first keepers, but the men returned home at the end of the summer. After their departure, the giraffe exhibit—and the subsequent installations at other British zoos, many of which received the offspring of the ZSL's giraffes—had few if any imperial undertones until the Scramble for Africa brought giraffe habitats under British control. By the middle of the century, however, an increasing number of British men were traveling to Africa themselves, and most were intent on hunting big game, including giraffes. Their experiences, widely read publications, and trophy displays made giraffes and other big-game animals into symbols of imperial conquest and control over Africa (see L IS FOR LION).

Giraffes are not dangerous, provided one remains far enough away to avoid their powerful kick, but they are surprisingly fast. This presented enough of a challenge for Victorians to consider hunting them sufficiently sporting. Several hunters found, though, that the thrill of chasing down a giraffe quickly gave way to regret as they watched the light fade from eyes that they found particularly expressive. A few even refused to hunt giraffes unless their entourage or local communities were in dire need of meat.

Other hunters felt no such compunction. In the mid-nineteenth century, they were not expected to, and were instead celebrated for their tremendous "bags." By the late 1800s, however, sportsmen had become some of the strongest advocates of conservation. While they had no desire to end hunting, they called for restraint, which was a relative term. Still, there were limits, and John Gardner Muir was criticized when he boasted of killing nearly three hundred large game animals in a four-month span in 1893. Sportsmen were particularly incensed by the dozens of rhinoceroses he killed. (Some said more than eighty, but he reported sixty-three). He also killed a baby giraffe and brought back the calf's skin and enough of the skeleton to have it mounted in the form of a chair.

A number of hunters in this era proudly displayed furniture or other useful items made from the animals they had killed, but Muir's giraffe chair was different because the informal sportsman's code of conduct discouraged killing young, immature animals. Victorians believed that hunting was a primal instinct, and that the overwhelming desire to hunt, felt by so many British men, offered reassuring proof that civilization had not made them soft. But hunters could not kill wantonly. They needed to spare animals—especially young ones—to guard against extinction and to demonstrate the self-discipline that they said set them apart from the so-called Natives they governed. Muir's chair suggested the hollowness of these claims, and it is likely that many disapproved of it. In many respects, though, the chair was a quintessential Victorian object. It reflected the popular fascination with natural history, the macabre, and so-called manly activities such as hunting, which were explicitly linked to imperial power and conquest. It was also one of the proudest achievements of the taxidermist who mounted it.

By the time of Muir's trip, decades of intense hunting and other pressures had decimated animal populations, including giraffes. When British colonies began passing conservation laws in the early 1900s, they often placed giraffes on the list of animals that were not to be hunted except under special license. Elites continued to encounter giraffes on glamorous safaris; and Britons at home still gazed at them in museums, zoos, and, by the 1910s, nature documentaries. In this context, giraffes seemed apolitical; they were specimens of science and nature. But the common image of them on open savannahs teeming with animals reinforced imperialist ideas about the primitive wildness of Africa—and the continent's supposed need for Western development and protection.

British displays of giraffes, both living and dead, illustrate the interlocking and sometimes subtle ways that imperial anxieties and assumptions filtered into the everyday lives of people in Britain. The Zoological Society's giraffe exhibit and hunters' trophy displays emerged from Victorian obsessions with the natural world and curiosities, but also reflected British assumptions of superiority and fears of imperial decay. The ZSL's interest in giraffes was catalyzed by the sense that French naturalists were besting them, and hunting trophies symbolized imperial power precisely because people feared that "civilized" Europeans were no longer manly enough to defend their empire.

The comparatively gentle giraffe did not, however, offer as clear a sign of British supremacy as more dangerous game. Giraffes' deaths could evoke discomfort for even some ardent hunters, but their appeal was effective in its own right. Imperial representations of and interest in these remarkable animals were not noticeably different than those seen in other times and places, which naturalized the imperial connotations. Giraffes continue to captivate audiences with their unique morphology and movement, and images of them in their natural habitats connect audiences with African landscapes that seem devoid of people and histories. In the nineteenth and much of the twentieth century, those aspects entangled giraffe representations with imperial rhetorics of difference and claims about the primitiveness of Africa all while seeming to offer a simple vision of one of nature's more unusual creatures.

Suggestions for Further Reading

Colley, Ann C. *Wild Animal Skins in Victorian Britain*. Farnham, UK: Ashgate, 2014.

Cowie, Helen. *Exhibiting Animals in Nineteenth-Century Britain: Empathy, Education, Entertainment*. Basingstoke, UK: Palgrave MacMillan, 2014.

Fitzgerald, William G. "'Animal' Furniture." *Strand Magazine* 12 (1896): 273–80. https://babel.hathitrust.org/cgi/pt?id=mdp.39015056049458;view=1up;seq=7.

Grigson, Caroline. *Menagerie: The History of Exotic Animals in England*. Oxford: Oxford University Press, 2016.

Holmes, Rachel. *The Hottentot Venus: The Life and Death of Saartjie Baartman: Born 1789—Buried 2002*. London: Bloomsbury, 2007.

Ito, Takashi. *London Zoo and the Victorians, 1828–1859*. Woodbridge, UK: Boydell, 2014.

Mackenzie, John. *Empire of Nature: Hunting, Conservation, and British Imperialism*. Manchester, UK: Manchester University Press, 1988.

Ringmar, Erik. "Audience for a Giraffe: European Expansionism and the Quest for the Exotic." *Journal of World History* 17, 4 (December 2006): 375–97.

Sharkey, Heather J. "*La Belle Africaine:* The Sudanese Giraffe Who Went to France," *Canadian Journal of African Studies* 49, 1 (2015): 39–65.

Steelcroft, Framley. "Big-Game Hunters." *Strand Magazine* 12 (1896): 437–48. https://babel.hathitrust.org/cgi/pt?id=mdp.39015056049458 &view=1up&seq=7.

Williams, Edgar. *Giraffe*. London: Reaktion, 2010.

G is also for . . .

Galapagos tortoise
Gazelle
Gharial
Goose
Gorilla
Gnu

H

is for

HORSE

If the horse is both a military and a transport technology, then the sight of cavalry mounts being transported across the Indian railroad presents something of a curiosity. On the one hand, horses were central to the establishment, expansion, consolidation, and control of British political power across the Indian Ocean world—from Egypt, East Africa, and the Cape to India, Malaya, and beyond. On the other hand, as this photograph reveals, horses also represented the numerous problems to be resolved within the imperial project. From the establishment of the East India Company's territorial and political power on the Indian subcontinent in 1757—the hub of British power in the Indian Ocean world—the British struggled not only to breed suitable horses but also to tap into existing trading networks. They faced resistance from merchants, rival rulers, and even the ecology of South Asia, and from imperial powers with whom they competed for warhorses across Eurasia.

Viewed through the movements of the policemen, soldiers, bureaucrats, and bankers whose activities took them from India to East Af-

....

Indian cavalrymen and horses on a train wagon, ca. 1910s. Photo by
Haeckel Collection/ullstein bild. Used by permission of Getty Images,
object number: 501379499.

rica, the Middle East, and Southeast Asia, the subcontinent was at the epicenter of the British Empire in the Indian Ocean world. But viewed through the lens of the nonhuman, such as the horse, India was at the periphery of empire(s). In all but a few areas of the subcontinent, there was a shortage of good fodder necessary to rear suitable warhorses., and a disease environment that dramatically shortened equine life expectancy. India's climate posed severe problems for Indian rulers requiring cavalry mounts. Given these conditions, India had historically been a net importer of warhorses from Iran, Central Asia, and Afghanistan through overland and overseas routes.

For the British East India Company, too, access to warhorses was critical to empire-building on the Indian subcontinent. From the mid-eighteenth through the mid-nineteenth century, they faced their rivals' large cavalry armies on the battlefield—Mughals, Marathas, and Sikhs. In 1796, the Company established a stud farm in Pusa in Bengal, under William Frazer. Thus commenced colonial experiments in breeding and veterinary medicine, motivated by both military and economic compulsions. The stud farm, however, was already struggling in 1807. Because its success meant the difference between safety and insecurity in India, a London veterinarian, William Moorcroft, was coaxed into replacing Frazer in 1808. The Company's demand for cavalry horses grew during the Anglo-Maratha wars of the 1800s–1810s, amid ongoing difficulty in improving breeding operations in Pusa. Through the 1830s and 1840s, wars in Afghanistan and northwest India exhausted the cavalry forces of the Company and depleted stocks of warhorses available across India.

Moorcroft traveled across the subcontinent, lamenting as early as 1811 the depletion of the better breeds, such as the Kathiawar, and the better breeding grounds and fairs, such as Butwal, Rampur, and Haridwar. What little trade there was with Afghanistan and Central Asia was monopolized by the Sikh rulers of northwest India, whose agents intercepted traders to secure supplies. Quality was also a problem. In 1819, Moorcroft left for Bukhara to source the finer breeds he had heard about from a Rampur dealer named Ahmad Ali Khan. The existence of these horses was corroborated by British Indian officers returned from Afghanistan, and by a "party of Northern Horse Merchants" who visited Pusa in the year of Moorcroft's arrival, offering horses which "in point of bone, muscle, temper and durability, are not expressed by any Race of Horses in the universe."

Moorcroft faced a series of disappointments on route from Peshawar to Bukhara, always convinced that better horses had been bought by local magnates or otherwise existed elsewhere. Some of Moorcroft's disappointment with the Central Asian (*Turki*) rested on its unfavorable comparison with the tall and agile English Thoroughbred—the creation of careful breeding between Arab and Turkish stallions and English mares over the seventeenth and eighteenth centuries. Yet Moorcroft's travels also revealed the extent of the transformation of Central Asia's horse trade, especially—to his disappointment—with India.

Central Asia was less of an interior periphery of the Eurasian landmass than a locus of the markets for military resources—such as horses—at the crossroads of empires. The tremendous pulse of empire-building from the mid-eighteenth century in Russia, China, and South Asia put pressure on Central Asian stocks. From the 1740s, Russia's procurement of warhorses shifted from the markets northwest of the Caspian Sea and intensified in the steppe farther east, continuing to rise as Cossack regiments were established across the Kazakh steppe from 1748 through 1867. Following the incorporation of Xinjiang into the Qing Empire during the Qianlong emperor's expansionary "Ten Great Campaigns" era (1755–92), the receipt of horses as tribute from Central Asia was transformed into more routine trade relations with Central Asian pastoralists. The horse trade continued at a reasonable level until the Taiping Rebellion in the 1850s.

India, however, was much more distant from the horse-breeding pastoralists on the steppes, and much more vulnerable to being crowded out of the market as the Romanov and Qing empires expanded. In this respect, the global dimension of British imperialism in Asia was much wider and more multifaceted than historians generally appreciate. If rivalry with France propelled British empire-building in South Asia from 1757, then the inter-imperial rivalry with Russia and China (knowingly or otherwise) for military resources in Central Asia acted as a check upon the pace and efficacy of British conquest, consolidation, and control of the subcontinent and beyond. It also transformed the Indo-Central Asian horse trade.

With the Company stud farm unable to meet requirements and a supply stream that was steadily drying up, the governor-general of India extended his search beyond the subcontinent around the mid-nineteenth century, turning to alternative networks and breeding grounds from the Middle East to Australia. Although there was well-established maritime trade in horses with the Persian Gulf, it was falling short of demand, and the governor-general desired information on how to secure the quantities and qualities of cavalry horses required.

Aside from freight costs and mortality rates, supply was deemed unreliable, however. The Ottoman authorities in the Persian Gulf prohibited the export of horses for a brief time in 1837. In 1866–67 and 1874–75, exports were limited to ten to fifteen horses. In 1883–84, the authorities resorted to stopping steamers and confiscating Arab and Persian specimens. Furthermore, this trade was jealously monopolized by Bombay horse merchants, mostly Parsis who had agents in Bushire, Baghdad, Basra, and throughout Southern Persia, and who resisted interference and competition from the Company.

Yet even within the British imperial web, securing cost-effective and reliable supplies remained a problem. Africa's disease environment, especially in areas plagued by trypanosomiasis (sleeping sickness), was even more of a barrier to horse breeding than India's. But empire is not a human endeavor alone. The demands of European imperialism in the competitive Indian Ocean arena motivated Dutch efforts to introduce and cross different breeds in the Cape from the seventeenth century, their aim to "produce" or "invent" a horse suited to this hostile environment. This project was continued by the British upon their seizure of the Cape Colony after 1806, making southern Africa another— albeit precarious—source of horses for the British imperial military in the early nineteenth-century Indian Ocean world. The horses' status in southern Africa not only as an alien species, but one introduced by the colonial authorities, was no barrier to its appropriation by Indigenous elites, however. In fact, the Basotho people used horses to build their offensive and defensive capabilities, to carve out a space for themselves in the new colonial economy, and to display their political status as part of their resistance of colonial imperial power—"how the empire rode back," as Sandra Swart so aptly put it in *Riding High: Horses, Humans and History in South Africa*.

In 1788, several hundred convicts arrived in Australia on the First Fleet. With them came horses—"animal migrants" forming the germ of an alternate breeding operation. Initially, land and convict labor were abundant and cheap enough to nullify the opportunity costs of horse breeding in Australia. With the flood of migrants during the Gold Rush of the 1830s, however, land prices rose, increasing horse-breeding expenses in turn. Nevertheless, the publication of the Indian Stud Committee's report in 1869 finally led to the inauguration of regular shipments of Australian cavalry horses. The suitability and cost-worthiness of Australian horses was continually in contention, and shipment quantities never quite fulfilled demand. Along with Australian, Arabian, and

Persian supply sources, therefore, studs would be established across the subcontinent in the late-nineteenth century in an attempt to meet demand in British India.

As Harriet Ritvo argues in *Animal Estate*, British concern with animal bloodlines and breeding mapped onto—where it was not directly in dialogue with—projects of making (sense of) racial and class distinctions. Beyond the metropole, more potently, the hierarchical ordering of colonial society was a shifting sand. It was as much tied to contemporaries' changing ideas about racial difference—and the extent of "progress" made by particular races from savagery to civilization—as it was implicated in these thinkers' crossings of the species divide. Just as the British shifted army recruitment from Bengal and Bihar to northwest India after the Indian Rebellion of 1857, they shifted horse-breeding operations from Pusa to Punjab's canal colonies. This move was underwritten by new ideas about the deficiencies of eastern India's ecology and races—whether human or nonhuman—relative to those from the northern borderlands.

From 1850, Punjab was thoroughly transformed under colonial rule, becoming a garrison state-within-a-state for British India as well as the British Empire in the East at large. Punjabi men, such as those in the photograph, were preferentially recruited into the Indian Army and dispatched on ships, much as Indian-bred or Indian Army–owned horses were transported to the theatres of British imperial wars around the Indian Ocean. There was yet another—too easily overlooked—"nonhuman" dimension to this transformation: some land in the newly created canal colonies was to be turned into stud farms to supply the military with warhorses. Ultimately, these operations were a failure. Whatever the belief about fundamental differences between Bengal and Punjab, the colonial authorities—military and scientific—faced the same set of challenges faced by Frazer and Moorcroft almost a century earlier.

The horse can variously be viewed as animal, commodity, or technology. The history of the horse, and of the horse trade with India and around the Indian Ocean world, highlights the complications faced by the British in establishing and asserting imperial power in Asia. First, there were the ecological and epidemiological conditions of the Indian plains that stymied indigenous breeding. Second, Indigenous merchants sought to maintain power over a profitable foreign trade. Third, rival rulers on the subcontinent or distant imperial polities—Ottoman, Romanov, and Qing—had a greater ability to procure and control supply in Eurasia. And fourth, new "horse" technology was appropriated within Indigenous African militaries. The sources of resistance to British imperial power were numerous and remained unresolved, as imperialists toyed with the same "solutions" time and again. The image of a string of horses transported by train, protected and preserved from the degrading effects of the Indian climate, is a reminder not only of the human and nonhuman networks and circulations that constituted the British Empire, but of the paradoxes inherent within the imperial project that so readily produced difficulty or disruption.

Suggestions for Further Reading

Alder, G., *Beyond Bokhara: The Life of William Moorcroft, Asian Explorer and Pioneer Veterinary Surgeon, 1767–1825*. London: Century, 1985.

Bankoff, Greg, and Sandra Swart, eds. *Breeds of Empire: The Invention of the Horse in Southeast Asia and Southern Africa 1500–1950*. Copenhagen: NIAS Press, 2007.

Caton, Brian P. 'The Imperial Ambition of Science and its Discontents: Animal Breeding in Nineteenth-Century Punjab." In *Shifting Ground: People, Animals and Mobility in India's Environmental History*, edited by Mahesh Rangarajan and K. Sivaramakrishnan. New Delhi: Oxford University Press, 2014.

Gommans, Jos J. L. *The Indian Frontier: Horse and Warband in the Making of Empires*. Delhi: Manohar, 2018.

Hevia, James L. *Animal Labor and Colonial Warfare*. Chicago: University of Chicago Press, 2018.

Metcalf, Thomas R. *Imperial Connections. India in the Indian Ocean Arena, 1860–1920*. Berkeley: University of California Press, 2007.

Mishra, Saurabh. *Beastly Encounters of the Raj: Livelihoods, Livestock and Veterinary Health in North India, 1790–1920*. Manchester: Manchester University Press, 2015.

National Archives of India (Military Department Proceedings), May 9, 1808, No. 87.

Ritvo, Harriet. *The Animal Estate: The English and Other Creatures during the Victorian Age*. Cambridge, MA.: Harvard University Press, 1987.

Swart, Sandra. *Riding High: Horses, Humans and History in South Africa*. Johannesburg: Wits University Press, 2010.

Yarwood, A. T. *Walers: Australian Horses Abroad*. Victoria: Melbourne University Press, 1989.

H is also for . . .

Hartebeest
Highland cattle
Hyena

I

is for

IBIS

The ibis is a nomadic and amphibious bird that travels in flocks and can traverse vast distances. Moving between land and estuary, the ibis wades and feeds in shallow swamps and marshes. Medium-sized, with long legs and a large wingspan, the ibis has a sharp, curved, and powerful bill as one of its distinguishing features: a refined instrument that allows it to extract mollusks, fish, and insects from watery environs. Typically found in warmer regions, the glossy ibis (*Plegadis falcinellus*) was first recorded in Britain in 1793. By the early nineteenth century, the sacred ibis (*Threskiornis aethiopicus*) was brought to France, where it became an important—though contested—symbol of modern imperial and racial science.

In the British imperial imagination, the ibis was in no way an extraordinary bird. Yet the sacred ibis animated some of the most critical debates of nineteenth-century imperial science in Britain and France: questioning the lines between myth, superstition, and reason (see also

....

The Ibis: A Quarterly Journal of Ornithology, cover image, 1859.

U IS FOR UNICORN); troubling imperial systems of classification; and surfacing in competing racial theories of human origins. If British imperial expansion was endeavored in part through modern science, especially the projected mastery of European man over nature, the ibis defied taxonomic systems and questioned the veracity of imperial knowledge. French naturalists mistook the ibis for the stork; Charles Darwin was baffled by the black-faced ibis (*Theristicus melanops*) and readily confused it with other bird species.

Of the twenty-six types of ibis, the sacred ibis featured prominently in imperial scientific rivalry and species debate. Following the sacred ibis takes us across time, geography, and empire. The first stop is early Egypt. "A notable characteristic of the Ancient Egyptians, which was absolutely incomprehensible to other nations of antiquity," wrote one correspondent in *Our Animal Friends: An Illustrated Monthly Magazine*, "was their love for the animal creation . . . nowhere in the entire *orbis pictus* of the ancient world do we find another people which took such care to domesticate indigenous, and to acclimatize, foreign animals." The ibis epitomized this adoration. With the aptitude to thrive in three of four earthly elements—water, land, and air—and as a sign of strength and wisdom, the ibis was celebrated in Egyptian mythology. Two distinct species—the sacred ibis and the northern bald ibis—made regular appearances in more-than-human cosmologies. Thoth, the god of wisdom and writing, was represented by a man's body crowned with the head of a sacred ibis. The northern bald ibis marked the hieroglyph for *Akh*.

Egyptian cosmologies distinguished between three realms: the earth, sky, and underworld. *Akh* was believed to manifest all three. In ancient mythology, *Akh* displayed superhuman qualities. It marked the horizon as a place of sunrise, renewal, and resurrection; was a mediator between gods and men; and inflicted punishment upon those who committed wrongdoing. The sacred ibis was a protector of life; the northern bald ibis was a defender of death. The former was credited for safeguarding crops by destroying real and mythical creatures: locusts, scorpions, serpents, and flying snakes. *Akh*, by contrast, was deemed a protector of tombs. Given their supernatural abilities, the ibis "rose to divine honors." The sacred ibis was routinely embalmed and mummified. This meticulous process of wrapping and preservation would come to shape nineteenth-century debates on evolution in France, Britain, and the United States. The ibis was at the center of inter-imperial struggles over scientific knowledge and territorial control and made regular appearances in racial theories of human origins.

In Britain, ornithology became a distinct field in the first half of the nineteenth century. Despite the efforts of naturalists to create a new scientific profession, British ornithologists relied heavily on Indigenous peoples and amateur birders in various parts of the empire (see also K IS FOR KIWI). In 1859, in further efforts to professionalize, the British Ornithologists' Union (BOU) founded what remains one of the most prominent journals to this day: *The Ibis: A Quarterly Journal of Ornithology*. The ibis became the official symbol of both the union and its journal. In the image they chose, the ibis is pictured as larger than life. It towers over Egypt, which is represented as a sparse and tranquil landscape featuring the iconic mummy, pyramid, and ruins. The bird is settled in the marshes, its regular habitat, and is turned away from the sun as it rises or descends into the horizon, possibly a gesture to *Akh*. As an imposing figure, the ibis is newly represented as the symbol of ornithology, a racial and civilizational aspiration of British imperial science and reason and its supposed triumph over the ancient myth, superstition, and sovereignty of Egypt.

Given their migratory habits, ibis were described by amateur birdwatchers and ornithologists as "staggerers" and "wanderers." In 1851, a poetic entry in the *Illustrated Alphabet of Birds* read, "I is an Ibis, who wanders in bogs, And lives upon lizards, and fishes and frogs." It was precisely the bird's nomadic qualities that made this species so difficult to identify, study, and enumerate. The northern bald ibis was believed to be indigenous to North Africa, the Middle East, and Central Europe. Yet some ornithologists argued that this particular species was never native to Egypt, despite its prominence within Egyptian cosmologies. The ibis could be found in Egypt, some agreed, but the region was a breeding ground and not its permanent habitat.

During the nineteenth century, the sacred ibis became an enigma for British and French naturalists and colonists. Was the bird mythical or real? Did it possess supernatural powers? Did the ibis really eat serpents and flying snakes? Was it indigenous to Egypt, or was this an error, made first in mythology and then repeated by European science? These debates carried high political stakes. They would be recast as inter-imperial disputes between France and Britain over Egypt as a place to be "known" and ultimately conquered. One objective of Napoleon Bonaparte's campaign in Egypt and Syria between 1798 and

1801 was to map the region, historically, culturally, and scientifically. By 1801, following Britain's defeat of France, a number of sacred ibis had already been sent to Paris for further study. The French naturalist Georges Cuvier argued that these species of ibis, venerated and mummified by the Ancients, continued to live on in modern-day Egypt. Following his examination, Cuvier insisted that there were no differences between the ancient and modern ibis. He used his findings to challenge ideas of evolution, especially those of Jean-Baptiste Lamarck.

Cuvier drew on the presumed fixity of the ibis to defend the theory of monogenesis (that humans originated from a single species) over polygenesis. His insights on the ibis traveled from continental Europe across the Atlantic. American naturalists invoked his findings to insist on a hierarchy of human species, and to support prevailing theories of racial superiority and inferiority. In *Types of Mankind*, published in 1854, physician Josiah Nott and Egyptologist George Gliddon extended Cuvier's arguments on the immutability of the ibis to support their claims on the unchanging character of the human species. Nott and Gliddon's theory offered support for slavery and for racial segregation in the American South.

The ibis found its way back to Britain through the writings of Darwin, in both the *Origin of Species* and *The Descent of Man*. In his famous voyage aboard the HMS *Beagle*, it was the "finch" and not the ibis that drew Darwin's attention. Unfamiliar with birds, he enlisted the assistance of English ornithologist, taxidermist, and friend John Gould. What Darwin identified to be "finches" were later discovered to be blackbirds or mockingbirds. Unlike Cuvier's ibis, Darwin's "finches" helped him to establish a theory of evolution that would have far-reaching consequences. Species, as he saw them, were not fixed. Rather, their traits and characteristics changed and developed over time and circumstance. In *The Voyage of the Beagle*, Darwin wrote, the "Ibis (*Theristicus Melanops*—a species said to be found in Central Africa) is not uncommon on the most desert parts" of Patagonia. "At one time of the year these birds go in flocks, at another in pairs, their cry is very loud and singular, like the neighing of the Guanaco." Just as Darwin confused his finches, he misidentified the black-faced ibis as an "African species." Despite his difficulties in classifying birds, Darwin's insights on continuity and discontinuity moved the debates of human origins away from monogenesis and polygenesis, the ideas that preoccupied his predecessors. His theory of evolution challenged and extended the scientific racism that animated taxonomies of British imperial worlds.

Despite its ambiguity, or perhaps because of it, the ibis has featured prominently in imperial iconography of various kinds. Mummified in Egypt as a sacred figure, the ibis was heralded as an object of racial science and taxidermy in France and Britain. It appeared in natural museums and private collections (see also L IS FOR LION), and animated the field of ornithology. More recently, the ibis has been reclaimed as a symbol of imperial disruption, as evidenced in Amitav Ghosh's "Ibis Trilogy" and in various signifiers of postcolonial independence. The scarlet ibis, for example, is the national bird of Trinidad and is pictured on the ten Dalasis banknote of The Gambia. Today, in continental Europe, the sacred ibis no longer incites curiosity but contempt as an invasive species. These birds, supposedly fugitives from local zoos, are believed to be responsible for environmental damage. The sacred ibis, which continues to feature prominently in Egyptian mythology, has resurfaced in parts of Europe as a foreign, unruly, and destructive ecological force.

Suggestions for Further Reading

Brown, B. Ricardo. *Until Darwin: Science, Human Variety, and the Origins of Race*. Oxfordshire, UK: Routledge, 2016.

Darwin, Charles. *The Voyage of the Beagle*. London: Penguin, 1989 [1839].

Devas, Father Raymund. "Birds of the West Indies." *Caribbean Quarterly* 2, 3 (1951–52): 39–43.

Farber, Paul L. *Discovering Birds: The Emergence of Ornithology as a Scientific Discipline, 1760–1850*. Baltimore, MD: Johns Hopkins University Press, 1997.

Illustrated Alphabet of Birds. Boston: Crosby and Nichols, 1851.

Jacobs, Nancy. "The Intimate Politics of Ornithology in Colonial Africa." *Comparative Studies in Society and History* 48, 3 (2006): 564–603.

Janak, Jiri. "Spotting the Akh: The Presence of the Northern Bald Ibis in Ancient Egypt and its Early Decline." *Journal of the American Research Center in Egypt* 46 (2010): 17–31.

Yesou, Pierre, and Philippe Clergeau. "Sacred Ibis: A New Invasive Species in Europe." *Birding World* 18, 12 (2005): 517–26.

I is also for . . .

Ibex
Iguana
Impala

is for

JACKAL
(AND DINGO)

In folklore across the world, the role of trickster has been filled by different animals. Fox, rabbit, and spider are perhaps the most well-known incumbents. In southern Africa, the jackal dominates this role. Whether *phokojwe* (in Sesotho) or *jakkals* (in Afrikaans), the jackal has made a powerful imprint on southern African folklore, a crafty little creature who delights in deceiving friend as much as foe. Whether outwitting the lion, humiliating the hyena, or duping Boer farmers (who appear rather like hirsute predators in such tales), jackals live by their ever-inventive wits. These various folklore traditions have also been mapped onto European tropes, as shown in an 1864 collection of Khoisan stories entitled *Reynard the Fox in South Africa*. This entry considers the jackal in southern Africa and contrasts it with the dingo in Australia.

....

"Desperate Encounter with a Jackal—A Man Seriously Wounded."

From *Illustrated Police News*, July 20, 1867.

War on jackals/dingos

Folklore may appear timeless, but the prominence of the jackal in southern African folktales can be read against a larger history of settler colonialism. This is brilliantly demonstrated by William Beinart in his article "Night of the Jackal," to which this entry is indebted. Jackals are found in Africa and Asia, but their prominence in southern African folklore can probably be traced to settler sheep-farming, which spread across much of the Cape Colony in the nineteenth century. Although there had been Indigenous traditions of small-stock farming with fat-tailed sheep for centuries, the settler pastoral economy dramatically increased the number of sheep. By 1865, there were eight million merinos in the Cape interior and southern Free State, areas that had previously been Khoisan territory or the borderlands of Xhosa, Zulu, and Sotho societies.

Unlike most predators, the jackal (*Canis mesomelas*) did relatively well under settler colonialism. Increased hunting made more carrion available, and settler small-stock farming augmented the amount of potential prey. Furthermore, the white settler presence upset the existing hierarchy of predators. In North America, settler agriculture aided the coyote by curtailing its enemies (the cougar and golden eagle) and competitors (the wolf). Likewise with the jackal. Its enemies and competitors, such as lions, were large, visible, and easily shot, as were packs of wild dogs. Hyenas' love for the carrion used in traps soon took a toll on their numbers. Nocturnal jackals, by contrast, generally hunted alone and relied on stealth rather than speed. Elsewhere in the empire, the dhole or wild dog (*Cuon alpinus*), a close relation of the jackal, did less well in the predator hierarchy. In southern Rajputana, the dhole was incorrectly assumed to be in competition with the tiger, prized by both princes and imperial officials. A bounty of twenty-five rupees was offered for killing dholes from the late 1920s to mid-1930s.

Small-stock farmers despised the jackal ("the pirate of the veld") and declared war on the species, hunting it, pursuing it with dogs, putting up fences, and using poisoned traps. Backed by state programs and subsidies, farmers formed poisoning clubs and hunting associations that shot the creatures for bounty and for sport. As noted in F IS FOR FOX, English-style fox hunts were recreated in different parts of the empire, using jackals in India and dingoes in Australia. The Cape was no exception, substituting jackals for the fox. One participant in a hunt praised the jackal as a "fox of foxes" with "beautiful action, smooth, subtle and gliding, stride for stride the exact counterpart . . . of his cousin of England."

As with dingoes in Australia, barbed wire and strychnine were favored weapons against the jackal. Yet despite this barrage of attacks, the jackal became ever more stealthy, learning to work its way around new methods of trapping and regurgitating bitter-tasting poisoned meat immediately. The Anglo-Boer (South African) War of 1899–1902 provided a brief respite. Fences fell into disarray, and agriculture ground to a halt; poisoning stopped, while opportunities for scavenging in the wake of the British army increased.

In the longer run, this assault on jackals may have proved counterproductive, as the wiliest and most adaptable jackals survived. As South African zoologist N. J. van der Merwe commented, "The old jackals, the diseased, the weaklings, the stupid or the young jackals [were killed]. The wary, strong and healthy jackals are not so easy to destroy. These, true to nature, will breed wary, strong and healthy jackals and the litters will usually be large. It boils down to this: that in South Africa we have bred a vigorous jackal." *Slim jakkals* (clever jackal) emerged not only as a character of folklore but as a historical figure and ecological actor.

Canine actors in other parts of the British empire were less fortunate, as the fate of the dingo indicates. In southern Africa, a diverse climate and ecology supported a rich range of fauna and hence of predators, with the jackal located rather low on the list. In Australia, the dingo topped the predator hierarchy (at least when European settlers arrived, other, larger predators having become extinct earlier on). Introduced millennia ago by sea from Southeast Asia, the dingo soon interacted with Aboriginal communities as pets, hunting dogs, and companions (and occasionally as food for humans). White stock farmers, by contrast, despised dingoes and declared war on them. They erected a fence, eventually 5,400 kilometers long (an "ecological Berlin Wall") to keep them out, and hunted, poisoned, and pursued the species to near extinction. In order to survive, dingoes acquired extreme stealth; those near human settlements learned not to howl.

The virtual eradication of the top predator reverberated across the Australian ecosystem, allowing rabbits, foxes, and cats to devastate small marsupial populations. The tide of conservation biology has started to shift, however. Its practitioners now encourage the reintroduction of the dingo, arguing that the species controls the cat, rabbit, and fox population, allowing small marsupial communities to recover. Wherever there are intact dingo communities, small marsupials do well.

Unsurprisingly, the representational life of the dingo has followed somewhat different trajectories from that of the jackal. For settlers, the dingo was vermin to be exterminated, a creature given to vicious cruelty (and baby-snatching, as the famous Azaria Chamberlain case demonstrated). Although dingoes were cunning, they seldom featured in settler mythology as tricksters; they came closer to portrayals of the lean and hungry, big bad wolf rather than the adept trickster fox. This ruthless wolflike image was invariably contrasted with the faithful farm dog, whose job was to protect the farmstead and pursue the dingo. The illustration taken from the British *Illustrated Police News* embodies this idea of the jackal as the disrupter of domestic and farmyard order. The newspaper was an early pioneer of melodramatic and sensational journalism; unsurprisingly, the setting of the image is not identified. The jackal had never been endemic to Britain, so the picture is somewhat confusing. Is this a rendition of a settler farmer from southern Africa or from Australia, with the dingo mistaken for a jackal? Or is the jackal an unwitting representation of a colonial disruption of the metropolitan social order?

In Aboriginal folklore, the dingo occupies an important philosophical role as progenitor of humanity—or, as the title of Deborah Rose's book notes, *Dingo Makes Us Human*. In it, she gives an account of a creation story that she heard from Old Tim Yilngayarri in the Yarralin region.

> In the beginning, when we came out of the ground, we had a long nose like a dog. Dreaming dog came around and looked, and reckoned, "Hey, you've done it wrong!" Long nose, big mouth, Dreaming was doing it wrong. . . . He didn't like his head like a dog. He wanted it to be round. He made a round one out of honeybee wax. And he called the little bat, that's the doctor, the little bat, and the bat said, "You come to me." He fixed their genitals up then— girls got a vulva, and boys got things rearranged. That's the beginning Dreaming that did all this. Same for women, same for boys. Now everything was good.

Just as the dingo fashioned human life, so too does it model death, as illustrated in the story "Moon and the Dingo." In this tale, Moon, which dies every month and returns, dares and taunts Dingo to do the same. Dingo reluctantly agrees to the wager but of course is unable to return, and so death becomes a reality for living creatures. As people are descended from dingoes, they too must die. Dingoes hence come to represent a universal history of humanity, linked to the mysteries of creation and the riddles of death. As Rose indicates, Aboriginal communities gave dingoes names, located them in a wider kinship structure, and lavished as much ritual attention on dead dingoes as they did on human corpses.

Folktales have always been multispecies genres, exploring the interaction of human and nonhuman animals. These stories are generally taken to be timeless and unchanging. Yet as the representational lives of the jackal and the dingo show, these creatures are ecological and historical protagonists who have shaped stories as much as environments.

Suggestions for Further Reading

Beinart, William. "The Night of the Jackal: Sheep, Pastures and Predators in the Cape." *Past and Present* 158, 1 (1998): 172–206.

Bleek, W. H. I., comp. *Reynard the Fox in South Africa; or, Hottentot Fables and Tales*. London: Trübner, 1864.

"Desperate Encounter with a Jackal: Man Seriously Wounded." *Illustrated Police News*, July 20, 1867.

Hughes, Julie E. *Animal Kingdoms: Hunting, the Environment, and Power in Indian Princely States*. Cambridge, MA: Harvard University Press, 2012.

Levy, Sharon. "The Dingo Dilemma." *Bioscience* 59, 6 (2009): 465–69.

Rose, Deborah Bird. *Wild Dog Dreaming: Love and Extinction*. Charlottesville: University of Virginia Press, 2011.

Wittenberg, Hermann. "The Boer and the Jackal: Satire and Resistance in Khoi Orature." *Critical Arts* 28, 4 (2014): 593–609.

J is also for . . .

Jabiru
Jaguarundi
Jellyfish

is for

KIWI

K iwi have had an angular relationship to the British Empire. Their unusual physical features troubled imperial science, confounding the neat assumptions of taxonomic orders. In the early twentieth century, the kiwi was fixed upon, appropriated by colonists, and mobilized as a symbol of nationhood. But while the kiwi's prominence in the symbolic repertoire of the nation has persisted, that process of meaning-making never erased or undermined the significance of kiwi within *te ao Māori* (the Māori world), in terms of both environmental understanding and cultural meaning.

Kiwi are highly adapted to their native habitat, where they faced no mammalian predators. With only vestigial wings and heavy marrow-filled bones, kiwi do not fly, making their lives on the floors of New Zealand's forests. They are the only birds with nostrils at the end of their beaks, and they use their highly effective sense of smell to seek out seeds, fruit, grubs, worms, and invertebrates. In each breeding cycle, female kiwi produce a single very large egg, weighing up to a quarter

....

"Apteryx Mantelli [North Island Kiwi]," by John Gerrard Keulemans. From
W. L. Buller, *A History of the Birds of New Zealand* (London: Van Voorst, 1873).

of the adult bird's weight. Their feathers are fine and dense, hairlike and bristly, lacking barbules and afterfeathers.

Prior to the arrival of Europeans, Māori valued kiwi highly. According to traditional narratives, kiwi were specially favored by Tānemahuta, the *atua* (god) of forests and birds. Some narratives identify kiwi as Tāne's eldest child, meaning that kiwi were in effect the older siblings of humanity, who were also Tāne's offspring. Other narratives explain kiwi flightlessness as a result of their willingness to protect Tāne by living on the forest floor and eating the insects that feed on trees.

Europeans first learned about kiwi not through the great scientific expeditions that made New Zealand known to the world in the 1770s but through commercial traffic in specimens and feathers, which developed as cross-cultural trade grew in the 1810s. The first such skin seems to have been traded by the Australian-based Captain Barclay, who commanded convict transport ships. Barclay sold it to the keeper of zoology at the British Museum, George Shaw, who named the species *Apteryx australis* in 1812.

Despite their flightlessness, kiwi effectively became more mobile as the islands of New Zealand were absorbed into the British Empire and they became the subject of naturalists, collectors, and traders. New Zealand was annexed by Britain in 1840, and colonial hunters were increasingly able to explore New Zealand's forests. They quickly discovered that they could gain high prices from a thriving international market for skins and feathers. This was especially true of kiwi species with smaller populations and a limited range of habitation, such as the rowi (found in the isolated south west of Te Wai Pounamu, New Zealand's South Island) and roa (great spotted kiwi). This market was a very significant driver of the marked decline of kiwi populations during the second half of the nineteenth century. In colonial New Zealand, there was also a strong trade in kiwi for both science and fashion. Sometimes the line between these domains of activity could be blurred. In 1872, for example, James Hector, the director of New Zealand's Colonial Museum, sent five kiwi skins to be made into a muff, presumably for his daughter Marjorie.

While kiwi were entangled in European fashion's global reach in the middle of the nineteenth century, their biology and appearance confounded British naturalists and classifiers. For more than two decades, George Shaw's specimen, stuffed and on display in the museum of the Earl of Derby, was the sole kiwi in Europe. In the late 1830s, three more specimens were sent to Britain by colonial collectors, feeding debate among an influential circle of naturalists interested in classification and the development of species. Professor Richard Owen's pioneering study of the anatomy of kiwi, published in *Transactions of the Zoological Society of London* in 1841, stressed the uniqueness of kiwi, emphasizing that they appeared as a "singular and seemingly anomalous compound of characters belonging to different orders of birds'"

From the 1860s, ornithology developed as an important domain of scholarly activity in colonial New Zealand (for ornithology in Britain, see I IS FOR IBIS). Much of that activity focused on moa—an extinct family of species of flightless ratites that grew to vast sizes. But colonial scholars increasingly understood that New Zealand's birdlife was unusually rich and quite distinctive, with a number of flightless species. Walter Buller's *History of the Birds of New Zealand*, first published in 1873, was key in shaping the colonial belief that New Zealand had the "most interesting and unique bird fauna in the world." The influential Dunedin-based zoologist T. J. Parker came to celebrate and identify with kiwi, arguing in 1891 that this "most anomalous and aberrant of existing birds . . . may be considered as one of the proudest possessions of our colony."

Despite the efforts of pioneering colonial conservationists such as Thomas Potts, no meaningful protection was extended to kiwi or other native birds during the nineteenth century. Potts worked hard to convince colonial politicians and European opinion-makers of the need to protect the fate of those birds, which he understood as "interesting aborigines" and "ancient indigenous forms." There were comparatively few public arguments made about the need to protect kiwi and other native birds from the demands of hat- and apparel-makers. However, there was growing concern about the impact of colonists and Māori who worked in the bush and treated kiwi as a game bird for food.

Buller, in particular, was an ardent champion for the protection and conservation of indigenous birds. He saw connections between the need to conserve native species and to recognize rights of Indigenous people. But those desires could be in tension. In the 1890s—in the face of strong arguments from scientists like Potts and Buller—the colonial government moved to establish Hauturu (Little Barrier Island) and Resolution Island as reserves. Resolution was a large, uninhabited island in isolated Fiordland. Little Barrier Reserve, however, was based on land compulsorily purchased by the colonial state, displacing the resident Ngāti Wai people in the interests of protecting birds. This measure was contested by Māori leaders such as Hōne Heke Ngāpua, the Ngāpuhi Member of Parliament who held the Northern Māori seat and consistently advocated for Māori political rights. Despite this opposition, the government appropriated Hauturu in 1894; the remaining Ngāti Wai people were evicted in 1896. Ngāti Toa leaders also fought against proposals to convert Kāpiti Island into a sanctuary to protect native birds, including kiwi. In stressing Kāpiti's central position in his *iwi*'s (tribe's) economic life, identity, and history, the Ngāti Toa leader Hemi Kuti, told Parliament's Native Affairs Committee that "the welfare and preservation of human beings should take precedence" over birds. From 1907, legislative protections were established to control the methods of hunting birds and to restrict the sale of meat to restaurants. During the 1920s, these measures were extended to give native birds full legal protection from hunting.

By that time, kiwi had emerged as a key marker of New Zealand and New Zealandness. That long process began in the 1860s, as colonists began to explore what made them different from their British compatriots. In 1865, kiwi were prominent in the design of the medals issued for New Zealand Exhibition held in Dunedin. The following year, kiwi were incorporated into the mace, a key element in the ritual and symbolism of the colonial parliament. From the 1870s, kiwi featured on Bank of New Zealand banknotes, anticipating the bird's prominence over the coming decades in imagery used by colonial insurance and banking interests. But it was the incorporation of kiwi into stamp designs that greatly amplified its currency as a symbol of the colony. In 1895, the postmaster general sponsored a competition to produce new designs for the colony's postage stamps, directing that entries should feature "a representation of characteristic or notable New Zealand scenery or genre." Kiwi appeared in a number of the submitted designs; a rather awkward-looking kiwi ultimately featured on the sixpence stamp, issued as part of the 1898 pictorial series.

That design and the everyday circulation of the stamp helped secure kiwi as a prominent marker of identity within and beyond New Zealand. But in the 1890s, a number of other native birds jostled with kiwi as symbols of colonial distinctiveness. At that time, moa were more commonly used in advertising. Other native birds were prominent in the 1898 stamp issue, including huia, kea, and kaka. Native birds, the use of Māori decorative motifs, and a selective engagement with the Māori language were important elements among colonial politicians, intellectuals, and writers, who put forth the idea that New Zealand was better understood as "Maoriland." This argument simultaneously recognized the centrality of Māori in colonial life and masked the violence and exploitation of colonialism; colonists were repositioned as an indigenized community distinct from Britons in the metropole.

Although some colonists were at best ambivalent about the idea of "Maoriland," in the first two decades of the twentieth century, a clear and recurrent set of national symbols emerged. In 1902, legislation confirmed the Blue Ensign with the Union Flag in the canton as New Zealand's flag. In the wake of the New Zealand becoming a Dominion in 1907, a new official coat of arms was created in 1911. Kiwi did not feature in either of these two key symbols, but by 1910, they had become a primary popular marker of nationhood. This shift was propelled by cartoonists, who used kiwi as a symbol of New Zealand rugby teams during the 1905 tour of Britain by New Zealand and the 1908 British tour of New Zealand. These images played with the inversion of imperial expectations and the established visual language of empire. The lion, representative of the imperial metropole, was far from rampant; it was bemused and battered in the face of the committed and aggressive, if unassuming, kiwi.

This visual language and its attendant cultural associations were reinforced during World War I. Colonial soldiers embraced the kiwi as a marker of their attachment to New Zealand and frequently called themselves "Kiwis." New Zealand soldiers etched this identification into the British landscape: at the end of the war, a large kiwi was carved into a chalk hillside above Sling Camp, where the New Zealand soldiers were stationed on Salisbury Plain.

Over the last one hundred years, constant repetition has reinforced the place of the kiwi as the key popular image of New Zealand's national identity. But that cycle of reproduction and reiteration has not altered the particular place of kiwi in the Māori world. Kiwi feathers are used on some *kahu*, the handwoven cloaks that are treasured by some *whānau* (families) and passed with great care between the generations. These cloaks, crafted by highly skilled experts, are potent symbols of leadership: they embody the mana—power, authority, charisma—of their high-status owners. Kahu *huruhuru*, feather-covered cloaks, are culturally significant, especially if the feathers came from prized species—particularly kiwis, as their fine plumage gives the cloak a distinctive movement. Kahu kiwi—like the cloak held within the Stevens Kāi Tahu whānau who descend from William Isaac Haberfeld—can be decorated with more than ten thousand feathers. The high esteem attached to such *taonga* (treasures) underlines the durability of an Indigenous symbolic system. It has persisted and coexisted with the recurrent deployment of kiwis by colonists eager to define their distinctive position within the empire.

Suggestions for Further Reading

Canadelli, Elena. "Authoritative Images: The Kiwi and the Transactions of the Zoological Society of London." *Nuncius* 30 (2015): 637–74.

Galbreath, Ross. *Walter Buller: The Reluctant Conservationist*. Wellington, NZ: GP Books, 1989.

Hunter, Kate. "A Bird in the Hand: Hunting, Fashion and Colonial Culture." *Journal of New Zealand Studies* 12 (2011): 91–106.

Hutching, Gerard. *Back from the Brink: The Fight to Save Our Endangered Birds*. Auckland: Penguin, 2004.

Palenski, Ron. *The Making of New Zealanders*. Auckland: Auckland University Press, 2012.

Sinclair, Keith. *A Destiny Apart: New Zealand's Search for National Identity*. Auckland: Allen and Unwin, 1986.

Star, Paul. "Regarding New Zealand's Environment: The Anxieties of Thomas Potts, c.1868–1888." *International Review of Environmental History* 3, 1 (2017): 101–39.

Stevens, Michael J. "'Pōua's Cloak': The Haberfield Family Kahu Kiwi." In *The Lives of Colonial Objects*, edited by Annabel Cooper, Lachy Paterson, and Angela Wanhalla, 252–58. Dunedin, NZ: Otago University Press, 2015.

K is also for . . .

Kākāpō
Kangaroo
Kite
Koala

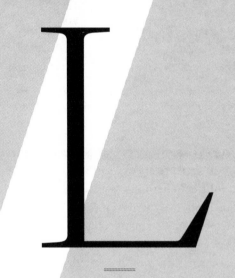

is for

LION

THE BRITISH LION'S VENGEANCE ON THE BENGAL TIGER.

T he lion is the most recognizable symbol of British imperial power in the modern era. Visible across a range of media—from political cartoons to biscuit tins to war propaganda posters—the lion is notable for his regal bearing; hence his association with the British monarchy. In many images, the lion wears the crown, and sometimes even an ermine cloak, as if to signal that the imperial nation-state and the natural worlds it sought to conquer were one and the same. He (for his masculinity is the condition of his embodiment) can often be seen holding a scepter and standing on top of an orb, fortifying the connection between monarchical rule and global power. So tight was the iconographic connection between the lion and British imperial power and ambition that imperialism itself need not be specified if the British lion was present. One of the most enduring examples of this association is the recurrent pairing of the British lion and the Russian bear. The image promoted the narrative of empires at war and called out geopolitical enemies, each ferociously committed to dominating the Victorian globe in animal form—implicitly imperialized. Empire need not even speak its name.

....

"The British Lion's Vengeance on the Bengal Tiger," by John Tenniel.
From *Punch*, August 22, 1857.

The lion conjured "might is right" by linking imperial power with the hierarchy of natural law in the animal kingdom. Britain's claim to global sovereignty thus seemed naturalized, its takeover of land, sea, and their attendant resources operating as part of a kind of interspecies birthright. The lion was a warning to local challengers or the enemies of empire. This might be metaphorical, as in the vast number of political cartoons where the lion threatens its enemies—Germans, Zulus, and even crisis-ridden English politicians. Or it could be literal, as when the *Missionary Herald* placed a statue of a bronze lion on its premises in Peking as "a terror to evil-doers." Not to mention the man-eating lion, capable of devouring his political enemies by taking their heads into his mouth. Here, the lion does so not simply to kill but to terrify into submission through a spectacular form of cross-species conquest—by ingestion, no less. Cartoons typically freeze-frame the onset of the terror, jaws opening and poised to crush, leaving little doubt about the stakes of tangling with the king of the jungle. The specter of commingling species contamination is definitely there. It is also present in the *Punch* cartoon "The British Lion's Vengeance on the Bengal Tiger," published during the Indian Mutiny: it materialized the overlap between transspecies and interracial anxieties in stunning form.

Unsurprisingly, the lion rampant was easily co-opted by critics and enemies of empire as hobbled, sleeping, skinnable, or past its prime. Colonial newspapers were fond of reversing the terms of debate, with articles titled "The British Lion in the Way" (of white settler reform); "Something the Matter with the British Lion" (for not reacting quickly enough to local threats); "An Eye Opener for the British Lion" (as he faces colonial realities on the ground). *Melbourne Punch* queried the "noble aspect" of the British lion by showing it devouring a kangaroo: a tale of interspecies warfare on the colonial frontier. In 1897, the *New Zealand Graphic and Ladies Journal* ran a cartoon depicting a lion with a Teddy Roosevelt mask trying to scare two Englishmen from a mountain path leading to Imperial Federation—suggesting how easily one Anglophone animal could assume the look of another to usurp global imperial authority. Empire less commonly bit back, but colonials could still threaten: one late 1890s New Zealand cartoon shows settler men getting ready to string up the British lion, crown and all. (See also K IS FOR KIWI.)

Beyond their lively geopolitical life, lions roamed widely across popular print culture in the nineteenth and twentieth centuries. As biggame hunting evolved from an elite pastime to a leisure sport and a tourist industry, adventure stories revolving around the animals' power and vulnerability appeared with increasing frequency alongside allegorical representations. Lion-hunting, in particular, was considered a rite of passage for a certain class of white manhood. Through its coverage in books and periodicals, authors and readers could participate in a development story about coming of age through the destruction of Indigenous communities—and embrace a sentimental fiction of love and respect for the "majestic dignity" of those they had annihilated. Narrators might express regret, without irony, about the fleeting pleasures of such activity in regions where the lion population was dwindling because of overhunting. As they explained, for the benefit of metropolitan readers, lion-hunting actually protected "Natives" unable to defend themselves from such predators on their livelihoods. These scenes are also occasions for glimpsing settlers' social relations, as they relied on local bearers to enable their expeditions. We see "Native" servants carrying and cooking. We also see tribesmen on the periphery, trying to resist the hunting party—not to protect the lion, but to mark the boundary limit of colonial incursion. There can be little doubt that lions were conflated in Victorian minds with Africa and vice versa. Together, the animal and the continent were seen as a test of imperial mettle. As one contributor to the *Idler* put it in 1909, lion-hunting in Africa was thrilling precisely because you know that "beyond you is nothing but savagery, far away from civilization, in primitive conditions, [and that you are] holding your position among Natives by the force of your own character."

This confident imperialism was tested, if not necessarily reversed, across the entire grassland biome that lions inhabited. The infamous case of the "man-eaters of Tsavo" (Kenya) offers one particularly dramatic illustration. Lieutenant-Colonel John Henry Patterson, an engineer on the Uganda railway, wrote a series of articles (later published as a book) detailing his "discovery" and subsequent determination to destroy two lions who were attacking railway workers. Those workers suffered gruesome fates: post-attack, we are told, "very little was left of the *bhisti* [water-carrier]—only the skull, the jaws, and a few of the larger bones and a portion of the palm with one or two fingers attached." The victim was not a white man but a laborer of South Asian origin, the keystone to the railway project who must be avenged. The number of people killed remains in dispute (Patterson claimed it was over one hundred) but the stakes are clear: man-eating lions standing in the way of technological progress had to be eliminated—which Patterson did, via a variety of high-caliber rifles. Though limits of space prevent a detailed analysis of this drama, what is significant is the prolonged struggle with the lions that Patterson recounts, and the decidedly unheroic tale he tells. Not only did he have to chase and shoot the animals over and over before they are stopped in their tracks; he could not have done so without his scout Roshan Khan, whom he grudgingly credits with saving his life by distracting one of the lions and allowing him to make the fatal shot.

This shambolic "win" is openly parodied by Maasai onlookers, who mirror back to Patterson his pathetic adventure—a pantomime that leads him to admit he succeeded more through luck than anything else. However else we read it, the fact is that the lions were killed and skinned, and their remains were sold to the Chicago Field Museum in 1924 for a tidy sum. Intended as a tale of derring-do, *The Man Eaters of Tsavo* also tells stories of struggle, reversal, near failure, and one small, fleeting win for the lion population. After he fells the last lion, Patterson goes back for the two lionesses who had accompanied them. He kills one but is unable to flush out the second. She escapes, leaving his total conquest undone. Though English and Indigenous women appear occasionally in such narratives, this is clearly the terrain of white man's power ascendant. The fact that this lioness gets away punctures that triumphalism, especially because she represents the reproductive future of the lion's kingdom. A fugitive, she is ultimately beyond the reach of this imperial hunter.

Because the lion was a major preoccupation of the modern British imperial popular imagination, it's worth noting that lions are not as easy to spot in other arenas of contemporary animalia. Lions are virtually nowhere to be found in Charles Knight's two-volume *Pictorial Museum of Animated Nature* (1844), and they hardly compete with monkeys, zebras, or cows as objects of scientific inquiry later in the century. As taxidermy specimens (see also I IS FOR IBIS), they were subject to a pseudoscientific method that allowed them to be viewed as curios in public and private spaces in the empire and at home. Given the frenzy of skinning and displaying animal specimens in Britain, you didn't need to be a lion-hunter in Africa to catch a glimpse of that signature imperial beast. You might just as likely see a stuffed one in country house or in public galleries like the Belle Vue Zoo in Manchester. You might also see a lion in the traveling menageries that roamed the English provinces from the early nineteenth century onward. Some of these featured lions and lion-tamers, the most famous being Martini Maccomo, colloquially known as "The Lion King." A sailor of African descent from either the West Indies or Africa, he was one of many Black lion-tamers whom native Britons would have seen from the late Victorian period through World War I. He often appeared in the full kit of the lion-hunter. He was so popular that Black lion-tamers who came after him were often known as Maccomo as well. When these men were covered in the press, they were as popular, if not more so, than the lions themselves—especially when they survived bites and other more serious maulings.

Meanwhile, as a reminder of how close the secular and the sacred were in British imperial culture—and how animals might mediate the social and cultural imagination in those domains—lions turn up frequently as object lessons in evangelical memoirs and stories. In these tales, Indigenous people encounter the lion and are scared straight into the arms of the waiting Christian missionary. Like the scorpion (see s IS FOR SCORPION), the lion is a cautionary tale about the perils of the imperial world without proper guidance and guardianship—and about the disruptions of and dangers to imperial zones of security always lurking at the edge.

Suggestions for Further Reading

"Black Lion Tamers in Hull and East Yorkshire." Accessed January 9, 2019. https://www.africansinyorkshireproject.com/black-lion-tamers.html.

Brian, Denis. *The Seven Lives of Colonel Patterson: How an Irish Lion Hunter Led the Jewish Legion to Victory.* Syracuse, NY: Syracuse University Press, 2006.

Colley, Anne. *Wild Animal Skins in Victorian Britain: Zoos, Collections, Portraits and Maps.* Surrey, UK: Ashgate, 2014.

Daston, Lorraine, and Gregg Mittman, eds. *Thinking with Animals: New Perspectives on Anthropomorphism.* New York: Columbia University Press, 2005.

Dufferwiel, Martin. *The A–Z of Curious County Durham: Strange Stories of Mysteries, Crimes and Eccentrics.* Gloucester, UK: History Press, 2014.

Patterson, J. H. *The Man-Eaters of Tsavo and Other East African Adventures.* London: Macmillan, 1910.

Ritvo, Harriet. *The Animal Estate: The English and Other Creatures in the Victorian Age*. Cambridge, MA: Harvard University Press, 1987.

Thompsell, Angela. *Hunting Africa: British Sport, African Knowledge and the Nature of Empire*. New York: Palgrave Macmillan, 2015.

L is also for . . .

Lemur
Leporidae (Hares)
Leopard
Lynx

is for

MOSQUITO

B ecause it can implant viruses and parasites into the blood-
stream of a mammal, the mosquito has been one of the great
concerns of empires large and small. In the colonization of the
Americas, yellow fever epidemics spread by *Aedes* mosquitoes were re-
curring impediments to Spanish, British, French, and Dutch settlers'
control of land and resources. Although Indigenous peoples were often
threatened by other diseases spread by colonial settlement, there are
repeated instances in which Native peoples and enslaved Africans
took advantage of immunity to yellow fever in order to challenge colonial rule. The most notable example is the series of military victories
against Napoleon's disease-stricken armies during the Haitian revolution, the first successful slave revolution in the Americas.

For British officials, control of mosquitoes and other disease-
transmitting insects became a significant environmental target by the
late nineteenth century. Insect control was increasingly viewed as necessary for expanding colonial development of agricultural and urban
land. It was also significant in the inter-imperial struggles for control of
populations and trade routes in Asia, Africa, and the Americas. Recur-

....

A health worker searches for anopheles mosquitos in Egypt, 1943.

Source: https://profiles.nlm.nih.gov/ps/retrieve/ResourceMetadata/VVBBFN.

ring disease outbreaks spanned the British Empire in the nineteenth century—including the great pandemics of "Asiatic" cholera crossing between India, the Middle East, and Europe. These outbreaks were one cause of concern that generated new investments in British colonial health institutions. As physicians and medical researchers learned more about the health effects of mosquito-transmitted diseases in the late 1800s, these insects increasingly were seen as tiny, mobile threats to a British sovereignty that vested rights in the property-owning, self-reliant male settler. British notions of the colonial right to Native-occupied land relied on the ability of settlers to geographically divide land and cultivate it using sedentary agriculture. Therefore, the ability to control migratory animal species and contain their threats to white control of property became significant to British colonial ideology and institutions. Tropical medicine emerged as a specialty, and the London School of Hygiene and Tropical Medicine was established in 1899. Public health officials in England developed institutions that devoted significant financial resources and personnel to controlling the cross-border transmission of parasites and viruses via mosquitoes. At the same time, British and U.S. health officials began to collaborate in developing new forms of insect eradication, as the U.S. expanded its overseas possessions in the Caribbean and the Pacific. By the first decade of the 1900s, tropical medicine was becoming an inter-imperial enterprise, with British, French, German, and American medical researchers collaborating across borders.

In the process, British and U.S. public health officials developed invasive strategies for mosquito control. In 1942, as British forces battled Nazi soldiers invading Egypt in the northern city of Al-Alamein, *Anopheles* mosquitoes traveled north from Sudan for the first time on record, carrying the *plasmodium* parasite that causes malaria. As they moved up the Nile River, aided by the construction of new dams and increased wartime shipping, the mosquitoes spread disease among a colonized population already facing the depredations of famine and war at the end of Britain's formal rule. From 1942 to 1944, 750,000 people contracted malaria, leading to the death of approximately 135,000 Egyptians.

The Egyptian malaria epidemic demonstrates how mosquito movements and behaviors are affected by the impacts of colonial land use on water and agriculture, the concentration of human settlements, the expansion of transit, and the basic health conditions of a given population. Mosquitoes were not always understood as the vectors of these diseases. Earlier in the nineteenth century, diseases like malaria were viewed as the results of filth. In England, the "miasma" of airborne dirt was often attributed to the condition of urban workers or rural peasants. But by the end of the 1800s, diseases such as yellow fever, filariasis, and malaria—which we now know are mosquito-borne—were increasingly seen as products of racial differences in personal hygiene. They were represented in racist terms by colonial officials and print media, who depicted these maladies as particular to the tropics: outcomes of poor hygiene, "backward" cultural practices, and unfamiliar climates and environments. What was often lost in such colonial discourses on disease was the simple fact that diseases viewed as "tropical" were often endemic within Europe and North America as well. Before it was known that malaria was transmitted by mosquitoes, famous works of literature, such as Charles Dickens' 1861 novel *Great Expectations*, suggested that malaria was a persistent concern within the British Isles. Dickens' character Pip was stricken with the malarial "ague," attributed to his rural location and his residence near the marshes of Kent.

But it was in the colonies that doctors discovered that mosquitoes were the transmission source of malaria from bodies of water to humans. Beginning in the 1880s, doctors working in colonial hospitals made advances in understanding the cause of malaria. In 1880, at a French-run military hospital in Algeria, Charles Laveran described the parasite that causes malaria. Soon after, researchers working in current or former colonies suggested that malaria and other parasitic diseases were mosquito-borne. These doctors included Carlos Finlay, Cuba; Ronald Ross, India; Josiah Nott, the Gulf coast of the United States; and Patrick Manson, China. Based on these findings, U.S. officials including William Gorgas, Walter Reed, and Fred Soper worked with the U.S. military and the Rockefeller Foundation, spearheading efforts to control mosquito-borne diseases around the world—most famously in the U.S. project to build the Panama Canal. By midcentury, mosquitoes were depicted as wartime enemies in health propaganda that compared Black, Asian, and Latino populations to mosquitoes.

By World War II, when *Anopheles* mosquitoes brought the malaria epidemic to colonial Egypt, malaria was one of the most significant factors in the outcome of military deployments across the world. The treatment for malaria at the time was quinine; Japan controlled much of the world's supply through its occupation of Indonesia. In this context, Reed undertook efforts to develop antimalarial drugs, while Soper carried out invasive chemical efforts to eradicate mosquitoes in Brazil and Egypt. Working with the Brazilian dictator Getúlio Vargas and the British colonial government in Egypt, Soper successfully advocated a three-pronged strategy to exterminate mosquitoes: use teams of eradicators to find, drain, and cover standing water with petroleum-derived chemicals to prevent breeding; control migration; and use DDT to treat humans and prevent mosquito bites. These strategies were invasive and relied on a strong state authority to impose control on often skeptical populations. Even then, they had to be adapted to local custom. This made DDT particularly useful, as it could be used on individuals without requiring clothing removal. This was important for ensuring its adoption in places where it was customary for women to maintain modest dress and to wear head coverings.

Control of epidemic malaria in Egypt required a large-scale deployment of health officials to identify, test, and chemically treat standing water sources to prevent *Anopheles* reproduction. Colonial public health involved training local populations in new forms of spatial surveillance, treating water sources as sites of risk. In carrying out such labor, public health officials were not neutral. They were engaged in practices of emergency intervention that intensified colonial surveillance of space and visually reproduced public divisions between British and Egyptian.

Despite the efforts of Soper, who was dubbed the "malaria dictator" in Brazil, colonial warfare against mosquitoes had limited success and high costs. After his departure in 1939, epidemic malaria continued in Brazil, as ecological and social conditions continued to bring populations in contact with open water and mosquitoes. Health officials succeeded in battling mosquitoes in Egypt in 1944, but once they tried to transport this result to other locations, it failed for a number of reasons. Chemical use had high costs for humans and the environment, *Anopheles* mosquitoes were present in higher numbers in other areas of malarial outbreak, and invasive eradication measures only work for a limited time period.

Soper's environmental warfare against mosquitoes reflects ways of thinking that divide humans from nature and society from environment. Such human-centered colonial thinking misses the complexity of bodies and ecologies that our contact with animals reveals. For example, mosquitoes have much to teach us about the smell sense. Scientists have identified a number of genetic smell receptors in the *Anopheles gambiae* mosquito that are attuned to chemical components of human sweat. Although not all mosquitoes bite humans to feed on our blood, those that do engage in a kind of airborne dance to identify and pursue us as their food of choice. Mosquitoes are less likely to spot a human by the visual identifiers we use—body shape, skin color, upright stance—than by the odors we emit. When walking along an urban path that crosses a creek-bed or sitting near a lake at sunset, human bodies emit chemical traces into the atmosphere—lactic acid, carbon, beads of sweat—catching the attention of mosquitoes that breed around water. Hovering in a cross-pattern while navigating gravity and wind turbulence, mosquitoes use antennae to identify the smell. They then estimate direction and speed of the scent trails that will lead them to the surface of our skin. From the vantage point of the mosquito, the human most likely appears more like a ghost than a body: a collection of gaseous plumes that linger and expand, coalescing in a hazy outline around the edges of the skin.

Millions of mosquito bites take place around the world every day. The bug barely catches our attention as we brush it from our faces, arms, or legs. Yet these moments of contact reflect a bigger story about the inherent weakness of a strategy that attempts to manage the colonized environment by viewing nature as an enemy—one that needs to be controlled by science, technology, and bureaucracy. The racist ideas that were used to justify British and U.S. colonization suggested that malaria outbreaks in India, Algeria, Egypt, Panama, and Brazil were the result of underdevelopment and poor hygiene. But the truth is that Euro-American development projects disrupted natural defenses against disease. Colonialism was the source of, rather than the solution to, malaria epidemics. When dams prevent rivers from fertilizing crops, they increase standing pools of water and the need for irrigation and fertilizer. When chemicals are used to control disease, they require dependency on the colonial industries that manufacture and ship chemicals. When doctors advertise that mosquitoes spread malaria, they encourage people to think of humans and nature as divided and at war. Colonialism undermined itself by ravaging the very nature that it sought to appropriate for profit. Mosquito-borne diseases today—from malaria to dengue fever to Zika virus—continue to dominate public health agendas, which suggests that mosquitoes remain effective travelers on the colonial routes of settlement and trade. Settlers were never able to dominate the environments they stole from Indigenous inhabitants. Today, medical researchers and health nonprofits continue to spend large sums of money on drugs, mosquito nets, and chemical repellents to oppose mosquitoes' evolutionary ability to smell, track, and bite human beings. The lesson, perhaps, is that mosquitoes are not our mortal enemies; they are products of the ecologies we create through forms of development that separate nature from culture, humans from the environment.

Suggestions for Further Reading

Ahuja, Neel. "Intimate Atmospheres: Queer Theory in a Time of Extinctions." *GLQ* 21, 2–3 (2015): 365-85.

Arnold, David, ed. *Imperial Medicine and Indigenous Societies*. Manchester: Manchester University Press, 1988.

Carlson, John R., and Allison F. Carey. "Scent of a Human," *Scientific American* (July 2011): 76–79.

Esmeir, Samera. *Juridical Humanity: A Colonial History*. Stanford: Stanford University Press, 2012.

McNeill, J.R. *Mosquito Empires: Ecology and War in the Greater Caribbean, 1620–1914*. Cambridge: Cambridge University Press, 2010.

Mitchell, Timothy. "Can the Mosquito Speak?" In *Rule of Experts: Egypt, Techno-Politics, Modernity*, 19–53. Berkeley: University of California Press, 2002.

Stepan, Nancy. *Eradication: Ridding the World of Diseases Forever?* Ithaca: Cornell University Press, 2011.

Worboys, Michael. "The Emergence of Tropical Medicine: A Study in the Establishment of a Scientific Specialism." In *Perspectives on the Emergence of Scientific Disciplines*, edited by Gerard Lemain, Roy Macleod, Michael Mulkay, and Peter Weingart, 75–98. The Hague: Mouton, 1976.

M is also for . . .

Macaque
Mongoose
Mule

is for

NORTH ATLANTIC
RIGHT WHALE

The world's oceans were not only traversed by imperial ships linking continents and islands; they were also zones for colonial extraction that included fish and sea-birds. And, from the beginnings of European expansion, this also included large marine mammals like the North Atlantic right whale. Beneath the seas that connected colonies with metropole, far-flung trading ports, and the coastal settlements of empire, whales formed kinship relationships within large migratory societies that became entangled in—and ultimately destroyed by—imperial forces (see also W IS FOR WHALE).

The North Atlantic right whale, a slow and ponderous surface feeder, inhabited the cooler northern waters of the Arctic and Atlantic. They fed and bred in the sheltered seas of the Bay of Biscay, the Davis Strait, around the northern Norwegian Island of Spitzbergen, and down the East Coast of the North American continent. Occasionally beached and periodically hunted by peoples indigenous to the shores it swam dangerously close to, it played an important role in coastal cultures. From the eleventh century, it also became an increasingly desirable source of critical and not-so-critical resources. Named for being the "right" whale to hunt, their thick blubber yielded rich supplies of oil used for lighting and soap; their baleen, which they used for feeding, was prized for its use in corsetry, whips, and umbrellas. They were so "right" that by the middle of the eighteenth century, they were almost

....

North Atlantic right whale (*Eubalaena glacialis*). From De Agostini Picture Library.
Used by permission of Getty Images, object number: 15001012.

extinct in western North Atlantic waters. Herman Melville's avenging whale in the mid-nineteenth century was the less desirable sperm whale, which became the focus of whaling attention after the near-total depletion of right whale populations.

Hunting for right whales was an integral part of British imperialism from the very beginning of its seaborne ventures. It was the Basques, however, who began commercial whaling in the eleventh century, when fishermen along the Bay of Biscay found an enthusiastic market for almost all of the carcass of North Atlantic right whales. These they could readily kill from small coastal vessels as the slow-moving giants migrated through the Bay from autumn to spring each year. As the trade grew, coastal right whale populations diminished. The Basques, now with larger seagoing vessels, ventured into more distant waters, arriving in Newfoundland by 1530. The profitability of right whale products did not go unnoticed by other Europeans. In 1607, Henry Hudson came upon Spitzbergen while searching for an Arctic route to China. The island had been disregarded by the Dutch a decade earlier as it offered no apparent profitability, but Hudson noted the abundance of whales in its bays and inlets. Seizing on the economic potential of Spitzbergen whales, the English Muscovy Company was granted exclusive rights by James I to whaling in its waters. It has been argued that the ultimate aim of this endeavor was to raise enough money to fund further searches for prized trade routes to China.

Coastal right whales were again beginning to decline in Spitzbergen and Greenland, with the growing enthusiasm of English and Dutch whalers and a deepening thirst for the wealth of products yielded by whale bodies. The low reproductive rates of right whales and the prolonged care of their young made repopulating after the violence of aggressive commercial whaling nearly impossible, particularly when mothers and calves were often favored quarry. Pre-commercial whaling populations of right whales are unknown, but many witnesses reported large groups feeding together in bays and inlets. Recent research on the emotional attachments of whales tells us that family members may have been reluctant to abandon their kin when under attack, staying close together rather than dispersing when faced with danger. Being slow feeders and congregating near the surface in large groups, their emotive behavior did little to disrupt the murderous efforts of colonial whalers.

However, even though whalers talked about the docile nature of right whales in comparison with the more aggressive—when besieged—

sperm whale, right whales did sometimes offer some resistance, particularly when their young were under attack. At these times, the strength and weight of their tails could cause lethal damage to a whaling vessel. More common for right whales, however, was a sudden dash toward the open sea when harpooned, towing the boat behind them. In 1812, Yorkshire whale captain William Scoresby wrote of a whale that pulled out six miles of rope after it was struck, pulling the boat under the water as it made its escape. But English whalers were not only dragged out to sea by desperate whales at the sharp end of harpoons; they were also drawn into marine territory described by the migratory, breeding, and feeding habits and cultures of northern right whales. The whales defined the reaches of Britain's colonial claims to ocean spaces by forcing whalers to "come to them" in their own oceanic kingdom.

Primarily focused on coastal whaling (rather than deep sea whaling like the Dutch), the English rapidly turned their attention to the whales that abounded along the New England and Canadian coast, soon after establishing permanent settlements in North America. With land harvests still scarce and unreliable, whaling offered immediate and dependable profitability. Drift whales—whales which had been beached, often during storms—had long been valued by the Native peoples of Cape Cod, Nantucket, Martha's Vineyard, and Long Island. They washed ashore so frequently that one seventeenth-century observer remarked that "no need had arisen to go to sea to kill them." But Britain's appetite for whale bodies demanded more carcasses than were offered up on the shore. Not only did British colonists decree ownership over beached whales; in their pursuit of profit, they pushed the territorial appropriation of eastern North America beyond the coastline, claiming proprietary rights to the sea and its contents. The ocean, as it reached out to the sustaining swells that supported right whale families and their extended kin, became an extension of the colonial space being claimed on land. That reach and those routes that colonial whalers took were not drawn or planned by men but were contrived by generations of whales whose elders were repositories of deep navigational and ecological knowledge.

It is estimated that from 1696 to 1734, between 2,459 and 3,025 right whales were killed in colonial North America. Many more were needed, as London installed five thousand street lamps during the 1740s. As right whale numbers sunk desperately low, their disappearance from the planet horrifyingly nigh, whalers were forced further and further into remote and dangerous parts of the ocean. From the nineteenth century, the Pacific, for a time, offered fresh quarry. But with the extent of the slaughter, right whale numbers in that ocean soon declined in a similar pattern to the Atlantic. All the while, amid the carnage, whales continued to set the field and name the time of battle. Their migration, seasonal cycles, and intergenerational habits determined colonial reaches into the northern oceans.

Today there are fewer than five hundred northern right whales left in the world. Although whaling has largely ceased (with the exception of continued Japanese whaling in contravention of the 1946 International Convention for the Regulation of Whaling) and right whales have been protected under the Endangered Species Act for several decades, there has been no observable population recovery. This is mainly due to fatalities from ship collisions, entanglement in fishing nets, and whales' inability to communicate effectively because of man-made noise pollution. The mass market and enormous profitability sought from whale bodies has also not ceased: now they are pursued not for oil but for pleasure. The whale-watching industry, a consequence of the successes of the antiwhaling and marine mammal protection movements, has become a $2 billion business enjoyed by over thirteen million people each year. It sells itself as way to see whales "in their natural habitat." But whale-watching has been shown to seriously disrupt natural behaviors, forcing whales out of their preferred feeding places as they seek to avoid the boats, which come as often as ten times a day. For surface feeders like the North Atlantic right whale, the boats that once decimated their numbers and drove them from their habitats now carry well-meaning tourists. Again, the whales set the stage and the place for their encounters with humans, but still their bodies are objects of profit and exploitation.

Suggestions for Further Reading

Adams Martin, Jennifer, "When Sharks (Don't) Attack: Wild Animal Agency in Historical Narratives." *Environmental History* 16, 3 (2011): 451–55.

Bolster, W. Jeffrey. *The Mortal Sea: Fishing the Atlantic in the Age of Sail.* Cambridge, MA: Belknap Press of Harvard University Press, 2012.

Bolster, W. Jeffrey. "Putting the Ocean in Atlantic History: Maritime Communities and Marine Ecology in the Northwest Atlantic, 1500–1800." *American Historical Review* 113 (2008): 19–47.

Davis, Lance E., Robert E. Gallman, and Karin Gleiter. *In Pursuit of Leviathan: Technology, Institutions, Productivity, and Profits in American Whaling, 1816–1906.* Chicago: University of Chicago Press, 1997.

Jones, Ryan Tucker. "Running into Whales: The History of the North Pacific from Below the Waves," *American Historical Review* 118 (2013): 349–77.

Perrin, W. F., Bernd G. Würsig, and J. G. M. Thewissen, eds. *Encyclopedia of Marine Mammals.* San Diego: Academic Press, 2002.

Roman, J. *Whale.* London: Reaktion, 2006.

Smith T.D., R. R. Reeves, E. A. Josephson, and J. N. Lund. "Spatial and Seasonal Distribution of American Whaling and Whales in the Age of Sail." *PLoS ONE* 7, 4 (2012): e34905. https://doi.org/10.1371/journal.pone.0034905

N is also for . . .

Narwhal
Nautilus
Newt
Numbat

is for

OKAPI

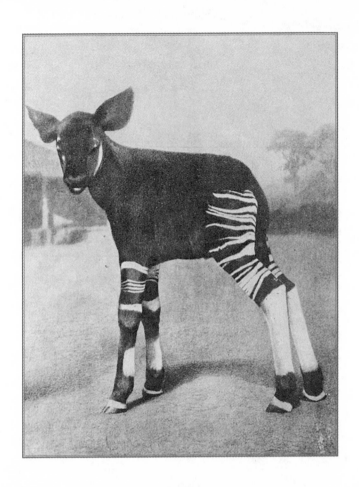

T oday, in the prosaic style of scientific nomenclature, the okapi
is defined as an "endangered, even-toed ungulate, family *Gi-raffidae.*" But this definition masks the fevered entanglement
of facts and fictions that evolved along with this elusive forest-dwelling
creature of central Africa. Okapis helped disrupt the orderly power
relations of the imperial exploration fantasy: the complacent, whig-gish narrative of discovery and classification, and a confident sense of
knowing. The okapi was discovered at the tail end of imperialism, the
last desperate scramble for an Africa of the imagination. Yet it fed not

....

"The First Photograph of a Living Okapi: A Calf about a Month Old."
From *Auckland Weekly News*, October 24, 1907. Source: Sir George Grey
Special Collections, Auckland Libraries, AWNS-19071024-14-2.

the hubris of empire, but its anxieties. It disrupted certainty and left an ambiguous legacy.

Africa has been viewed as the source and home of animals for at least two millennia. The continent's stereotype as a prelapsarian wilderness has inspired global imaginings. It has been deemed a placeless space to project fantasies from the self-considered center (be it the metropoles of Rome, Constantinople, Basra, Lisbon, or London). This brings us to what could be called the "okapi fallacy," which follows the muddled story of the "discovery" of the okapi itself. The fallacy is the result of an imperial gaze—the Eurocentric/Global North perspective—that posits a raw African "nature" waiting to be discovered and classified by outside scientists. Thus it was with the okapi; but the story was more complicated than that. The okapi was recognized—perhaps even by the ancient Egyptians—and was part of a far older imperial network. Okapis were depicted on a frieze of a procession of delegates paying homage to Xerxes in the early fifth century BCE. It shows a parade of pygmies leading a tamed okapi by a bridle. This okapi had traveled three thousand miles from central Africa to the Mediterranean world.

To the Indigenous peoples who lived in the same central African forests, the okapi was well known. Europeans, however, did not believe early whispers, dubbing the creature the "African Unicorn." By the 1870s stories of the creature hit the west. The rumors were fueled by a Russian adventurer, Wilhelm Junker, who explored the Congo between 1882 and 1886. When Henry Morton Stanley was pottering with his porters in the Ituri Forest, he became interested in the local term "okapi" (which he misheard and wrote down as *"atti"*) uttered by the M'buti (or Bambuti) pygmies when they saw his expedition's horses; he had been surprised by their *lack* of surprise on seeing his horses. He questioned them and learned of a secretive forest horse, which they sometimes managed to catch and consume by trapping it in hunting pits deep in the forest. Stanley excitedly spread the word of this mysterious new horse. (The M'buti probably nodded wearily and tried to explain to Stanley that this was not exactly news to them.) In 1890, Stanley popularized the ancient trope of *ex africa semper aliquid novi* ("out of Africa, always something new")—or *equid novi* ("new horse")—in a best-selling book about the silent, gloomy forests and their secrets. It sold 150,000 copies in English and was translated into other languages, and it gave Ituri the enduring label "Darkest Africa."

Stanley's account fell into the hands of Harry Johnston, explorer and colonial administrator, who became obsessed with discovering this strange creature. To him it became a kind of unicorn of the late imperial age, epitomizing the last vestiges of unknown and unconquered nature. He hypothesized and fantasized about its identity in equal parts: Was it an undiscovered species of forest zebra? Or, more tantalizingly, perhaps even a prehistoric Hipparion protohorse, a "missing link" between modern and ancient equines? Johnston, who was himself (as his obituarist observed) something of a "living link" between the nineteenth-century explorers and the "more scientific investigation" of the twentieth century, organized a dedicated expedition to find the creature. Some have called it—on a metaphorical level—the "last great unicorn hunt." This equine of the dark, dappled forests was even said to sport horns. Johnston heard the M'buti call it a slightly different name, the inflected and drawn out "*o'api*," which might simply have been a M'buti plea to "stop badgering us about this beast." When they finally showed Johnston the cloven-hoofed tracks on a forest path, he dyspeptically damned the "Natives" for trying to hoodwink him: he had been expecting horse hoofprints. Not unexpectedly, with his blinkered view (as it were) he left without ever seeing an actual okapi.

However, he did secure bits and pieces of the bodies of okapis—a jawbone, a skull, cloven hooves, and two bandoliers (traditional headbands) made of okapi skin—which he treasured like relics. An outline was being filled in—although he could not yet hope to fathom the rich, dark-purpled gloss of their coats, their large brown eyes, their unique striping, their fawn-faced beauty. But he diligently gathered their bones and sent this animal reliquary to the Zoological Society of London to be classified. An enduring debate erupted: some considered the enigmatic quadruped to be a "kind of degenerate giraffe." In early 1901, the creature was baptized—with a curious mixture of restraint and bombast— "*Equus (?) johnstoni*." The "equus" appellation referred to Johnston's belief that it must be essentially a horse. A few months later, he was sent a skin and skulls by a Swedish officer and had to concede that the okapi was more like a giraffe. He then quite modestly suggested the name *Helladotherium tigrinum* (the first word was a reference to an ancient extinct giraffe and the second was an allusion to its tigerlike stripes). The director of the British Museum, however, firmly renamed it "*Okapia johnstoni*"—which remains its accepted taxonomic nomenclature. In 1903, it was declared a brand-new genus, a new species.

An animal new to western science at the start of the twentieth century was a wonder. There was a scramble to obtain this rare prize. The Belgians finally captured one for the Antwerp Zoo, but only after World

War I in 1919. It made newspapers around the world and led to a heated taxonomic debate. Was it a "primitive giraffe," a primeval giraffid, a living fossil that had somehow survived from the Miocene? (After all, a living coelacanth had been discovered by the 1930s and such fevered discussions were loaded with meaning.) Was it a degenerate giraffe, one that had evolved too far? Or was it a highly evolved, specialized secondary forest inhabitant? Many of the arguments centered on the horns or "ossicones." Were they simply "truly primitively small" or were they "degenerate"? In essence, were they the alpha or omega? This resonated with late imperial discussions over Okapis' fellow forest-dweller, the pygmies: were they innocent primordial "living fossils," or were they degenerate humans, too long allowed to develop in the dank, dark recesses? By 1938, Edwin Colbert heralded the okapi as one "of the most exciting events in the history of modern mammalogy."

Okapis achieved iconic status and wide popular visibility. Protected by law from 1933, they appeared on banknotes of the Congolese franc, as the logo on the national conservation agency, as the eponymous entity in a World Heritage Site (the Okapi Wildlife Reserve), and as a brand of "Okapi" cigarettes. Yet they remained little-studied and elusive beasts. They were creatures of the liminal spaces, nibbling at the edges of "scientific knowledge" in an area too vast, too far, or too bellicose to study in depth. Their habits and habitat have made okapis hard to observe in the wild. Yet they can be hidden in plain sight. In Virunga National Park, for example, they were feared extinct for fifty years, but were there all along. The last recorded sighting of an okapi in the Watalinga Forest was in 1959, but it was suddenly seen happily browsing in 2006 as part of a thriving but unnoticed community. They were initially hard to keep alive, and the first birth in captivity was only in 1954. They emit noises too low for the human ear to pick up. They retain an obvious similarity to giraffes, from their long, licorice-colored tongues to their peculiar gait, moving simultaneously with front and hind on the same side. Their very bodies are inexplicable. Modern analysis has revealed that they split from giraffes about sixteen million years ago, becoming highly specialized and limited to the rainforests of central and northeastern Democratic Republic of the Congo. Yet, oddly, they retained a very high genetic variation. Not all okapis even have the same number of chromosomes.

In the story of the okapi, the ambiguities of power remain. It takes its official name from a servant of empire who never saw a living okapi. On the other hand, its common name is a vernacular word from an otherwise globally voiceless people. And from the mid-twentieth century mark, okapi assumed a new role in popular global iconography: they became the symbol of cryptozoology. This is the study of the fringes of zoology (somewhere between twentieth-century exploration and pseudoscience). Its enthusiasts try to find proof of a continuum of creatures from Bigfoot to living dinosaurs. For them, okapis disrupted the stale imperial narrative that "everything is discovered and classified and *known*." The International Society of Cryptozoology adopted the okapi as symbol, redrawn from a photograph of a baby okapi. Along with animals like the mountain gorilla and Komodo dragon (discovered by the "west" in 1902 and 1912 respectively) the okapi represents folklore come alive. In a world that is too well mapped and too well tracked, it inspires a sense of wonder. For cryptozoologists, the okapi is more than an animal: it is hope embodied.

Suggestions for Further Reading

Colbert, Edwin H. "The Relationships of the Okapi." *Journal of Mammalogy* 19, 1 (1938): 47–64.

Dreyer, Tom. *Equatoria*. Translated by Michiel Heyns. Chicago: Aflame, 2008.

Johnston, H. H. "A Monograph of the Okapi." *Nature* 85 (1910): 209–211.

Kingsolver, B. *The Poisonwood Bible*. New York: Harper, 1998.

Lankester, E. Ray. *A Monograph of the Okapi*. Compiled by W. G. Ridewood. London: British Museum, 1910.

Lavers, Chris. *The Natural History of Unicorns*. New York: Morrow, 2009.

Lindsey, Susan Lyndaker, Mary Neel Green, and Cynthia L. Bennett. *The Okapi: Mysterious Animal of Congo-Zaire*. Austin: University of Texas Press, 1999.

Putnam, P. "There is Such an Animal." In *Through Hell and High Water*, edited by Seward S. Cramer. New York: R. M. McBride, 1941.

Schlein, Miriam. *On the Track of the Mystery Animal: The Story of the Discovery of the Okapi*. New York: Four Winds, 1978.

Shuker, K. *The Lost Ark: New and Rediscovered Animals of the Twentieth Century*. London: Harper Collins, 1993.

Weidensaul, Scott. *The Ghost with Trembling Wings: Science, Wishful Thinking and the Search for Lost Species*. New York: North Point, 2002.

O is also for . . .

Ocelot
Octopus
Orangutan
Otter

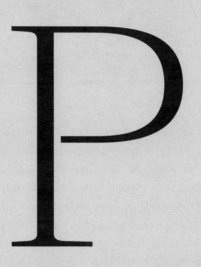

P

is for

PLATYPUS

I f ever there was an animal that seemed designed to confound,
perplex, and upset colonial science, it was the humble platypus
(*Ornithoryhnchus anatinus*). Often described as "paradoxical," the
duck-billed, web-footed, beaver-tailed mammals seemed to invert the
order of nature. They combined the features of so many animals that
it boggled the imagination. A young Charles Darwin said of the platypus that "A Disbeliever in everything beyond his own reason, might
exclaim, 'Surely two distinct Creators must be at work.'" British scientists' obsession with the delicate matter of the platypus's reproduction (in particular, whether or not it laid eggs and nursed its young)
illustrated some of the profound tensions at the heart of imperial
science—that is, the relative authority of amateurs and professionals,
the cabinet and field, and Indigenous people and colonial laymen.

When the first desiccated specimens of dead platypus made their
way to Europe in the late eighteenth century, some thought that they
must be an elaborate joke perpetrated by unscrupulous taxidermists.
Thomas Bewick wrote in 1800 that, "it seems to be an animal *sui ge-
neris*; it appears to possess a threefold nature, that of a fish, a bird, and

....

"Duck-Billed Platypus," by Louisa Anne Meredith. From *Tasmanian Friends
and Foes: Feathered, Furred and Finned* (London: Day, 1880). Courtesy of State
Library of Tasmania.

a quadruped, and is related to nothing that we have hitherto seen." Indeed, the little creature defied all existing classification systems for ordering nature and thus making sense of new lands, peoples, and animals. Platypus were furry, like mammals, but their reproductive organs looked more like a those of a bird or a reptile. Both the platypus and echidna are monotremes, referring to their cloaca, a single opening for excretory, urinary and reproductive functions., One delicate naturalist deemed this "highly curious, but not well adapted for popular details." Females had no nipples, but they had mammary glands, though this was a point of considerable debate (the famous French naturalist Étienne Geoffroy Saint-Hilaire once wrote, "If those are mammary glands, where is the butter?"). In fact, the milk leaks through the mother's skin, where babies whose beaks are not yet fully formed lap it up. Males had a poisonous spur on the insides of their hind legs that, extruded a powerful venom, causing excruciating pain to anyone so unfortunate as to be "spiked." Most of all, there was the question of reproduction: were platypus oviparous (egg-laying), viviparous (giving birth to live young), or ovoviviparous (young hatching from eggs within the mother's body)? And if these bizarre animals could be mammals, what did that say for the stability—or indeed, the legitimacy— of the classifications of the natural world that western science depended upon? Members of the newly founded Philosophical Society of New South Wales lamented in their journal in 1821 that "We are almost inclined to believe that Nature has been leading us through a mazy dance of intellectual speculation, only to laugh at us at last in this fifth continent."

The obsession of male scientists with the reproductive habits of female platypus eclipsed many of the other questions about this extraordinary animal, including the strange poisonous spurs on the male's hind legs. Solving the question of whether or not the platypus laid eggs became a holy grail of nineteenth-century science. Like the animals themselves, the answer proved elusive, particularly because the testimony of those who knew it most intimately—Aboriginal informants— was given little weight. Hundreds of animals were sent to naturalists around the world as pickled, dried, packed in barrels of salt or alcohol. Naturalists in hot pursuit of platypus eggs relied heavily on Aboriginal assistance to navigate and to survive in unknown territory. They also relied on Indigenous knowledge, quizzing guides, hunters, and translators for clues to how to find and catch nesting animals. A plethora of Aboriginal accounts of the mammals laying eggs and suckling their young were published in travel narratives and in the journals of colonial scientific societies. Aboriginal explanations of the secretive platypus's biology and behavior filtered into the vernacular poetry, song, and story of white settlers, but the perception remained that Aborigines were unreliable witnesses. Many of naturalist George Bennet's contemporaries fully endorsed his statement that "On the whole we may infer that no dependence can be placed on native accounts, but that naturalists must seek for information in their own investigations."

The odd little mammal was harnessed to colonial ambitions in more ways than one, becoming an unlikely vessel for white settlers' search for respectability. Australian scientific societies were deeply interested in the strange flora, fauna, and geology of the Australian continent. But they were several months' sail away from Britain and the Cape; their libraries were small and their members isolated. The Tasmanian Society of Natural History, established in 1839, took the platypus as its emblem; its Latin motto was *Quocunque aspicias hic paradoxus erit* ("From wherever you look at it, this will be a paradox"). Part of the Society's goal was to enhance the colony's reputation with both influential men of science and the British public. It sought to demonstrate that the free settlers of the penal colony of Van Diemen's Land (Tasmania) were urbane, civilized, and untainted by either the sizeable population of convicts or by their own history—particularly the war of extermination that the settlers had perpetrated against Tasmanian Aborigines in the 1820s and 1830s. The *Tasmanian Journal*— or as its founder Lady Jane Franklin called it, "My Platipus Society"—solicited contributions on all scientific subjects from around the world. Its patroness ensured that it got wide distribution from its distinguished London publisher, John Murray. The Tasmanian naturalist Louisa Anne Meredith also used the enigmatic platypus to advertise the colony's advantages and defend its dark past, all within the context of her colonial home. In her beautifully illustrated 1881 book, *Tasmanian Friends and Foes: Feathered, Furred and Finned*, she combined her children's sentimentalized accounts of playful platypuses frolicking in sparkling Tasmanian rivers with her husband's reminiscences about the "Black War." These included his defense of the colonists' genocidal campaign against Tasmanian Aborigines, and his bald statement that the Aborigines were "the very lowest type of humanity; the ugliest, least intelligent, and least teachable of savages."

Metropolitan scientists were circumspect at best, and suspicious at worst, about both the quality of field observations (especially if they came from Aboriginal sources) and about the competence of colonial naturalists. In the eyes of the powerful naturalist Robert Owen and others, the only way to solve the problem of platypus generation was through a mountain of platypus bodies, until one dead animal could definitively prove whether or not the animals laid eggs. It was not until 1884 that the platypus's secret was officially "discovered." William Caldwell, a Scottish embryologist from Cambridge University, had come to Queensland to study the platypus and lungfish (both of which were considered to be "living fossils). Employing more than a hundred Indigenous hunters, Caldwell presided over the slaughter of hundreds of echidna and platypus in the search for their eggs. In late August, he finally shot a female whose first egg had been laid, with a second one at the mouth of her uterus. He then sent a famous telegram from the Queensland frontier to the British Association for the Advancement of Science (meeting for the first time in Montreal) declaring, "Monotremes oviparous, ovum meroblastic:" monotremes lay eggs, and that the eggs they lay are like those of a bird.

The platypus's secrets might rocket around the world—and so might its mortal remains—but the living animal itself was not a traveler. The secretive platypus forms labyrinthine burrows in and along the banks of the rivers, in which mothers make their nests, lay their eggs, and nurse their babies, and which would-be hunters have to laboriously dig up. In the early twentieth century, the self-taught naturalist Harry Burrell developed what he called the "platypusary"—a complicated artificial burrow complete with running water, allowing the platypus to truly have a mobile home away from home. The first living platypus were displayed at Sydney Zoological Gardens in 1910, followed by six who made the long voyage to New York in 1922.

The platypus remains both elusive and ubiquitous in Australia. Though most residents have never seen one (their habitats are increasingly threatened by urban expansion, agricultural, and mining practices), they handle them every day—on their twenty-cent piece. Like the early platypus specimens, these little tokens circulate around the continent and around the world, carrying messages that are important to outsiders, but totally irrelevant to Old Man Platypus.

Suggestions for Further Reading

Hobbins, Peter. "A Spur to Atavism: Placing Platypus Poison." *Journal of the History of Biology* 48, 4 (2015): 499–537.

Jenkins, Bill. "The Platypus in Edinburgh: Robert Jameson, Robert Knox and the Place of the *Ornithorhynchus* in Nature, 1821–24." *Annals of Science* 73, 4 (2016): 425–41.

Kemp, Martin. "'The Testimony of My Own Eyes': The Strange Case of the Mammal with a Beak." *Spontaneous Generations: A Journal for the History and Philosophy of Science* 6, 1 (2012):43–49.

Moyal, Ann. *Platypus: The Extraordinary Story of How a Curious Creature Baffled the World*. Sydney: Allen and Unwin, 2001.

Ritvo, Harriet. *The Platypus and the Mermaid, and Other Figments of the Classifying Imagination*. Cambridge, MA: Harvard University Press, 1997.

P is also for . . .

Panther
Peacock
Penguin
Polar Bear
Python

is for

QUAGGA

T he most significant thing about the quagga may have been its disappearance, because at first there were so many of them. Their numbers featured prominently in early descriptions. For example, in his *History of Quadrupeds*, eighteenth-century naturalist Thomas Pennant noted that quaggas lived in vast herds, like the common zebras they closely resembled. He carefully distinguished the two kinds, however. Physically, quaggas were stockier and more modestly striped. Morally, quaggas were braver, inclined to attack marauding hyenas, and at the same time more docile and tameable, as if designed by nature as "the beast of draft or of burden" for southern Africa. A century later, the analogous entry in *The Royal Natural History* regretfully described these vast quagga populations in the past tense: although the herds had still been characterized as "immense" in the 1830s, over the intervening decades they had "been completely or very nearly exterminated." As it turned out, even this gloomy accounting was optimistic. It is difficult to pinpoint the demise of the final members of a diminish-

....

"Quagga in enclosure, with keeper," 1861. Photo by Frank Haes.
Courtesy of Zoological Society of London.

ing species, but subsequent consensus has put the extinction of free-living quaggas in the 1870s. Over the years, a small stream of quaggas had trickled into European private menageries and public zoos; the last captive quagga died in Amsterdam in 1883.

The reasons for the quagga's disappearance were not obscure. They had not been prized as game animals or trophies, so colonial sportsmen could not be blamed. Instead, the quagga had succumbed to a combination of economic pressures. For several centuries, farmers in the Cape region had hunted them to provide food for African farm laborers. As settler agriculture expanded into quagga habitat, they were eliminated as unwelcome competitors with domestic livestock. During the nineteenth century, a commercial market also developed for their hides. Despite these multi-pronged assaults, quagga herds apparently remained vast for some time. Then suddenly, or so it seemed, they were gone.

By this time, the mere fact of extinction had ceased to surprise, and doubts about its theological possibility (cognate with current creationist concerns about evolution) had been laid to rest. The quagga was far from the first animal to disappear after close encounters with European adventurers or settlers. During the seventeenth century, the dodo had vanished from Mauritius; a century later, the Steller's sea cow had disappeared from the North Pacific. By the end of the eighteenth century and much closer to quagga habit, the bluebuck—a kind of antelope—had been hunted to extinction by Cape settlers. But these species were understood to have relatively small populations and limited ranges. Sportsmen throughout the British Empire had also begun to realize that in the areas that they frequented most heavily, their targets were apt to become scarce. However, they tended to attribute this increasing rarity to the game animals' prudent decision to retreat to less exposed locations, rather than to their own enthusiastic predation.

What made the likely (and, soon afterward, certain) extinction of the quagga particularly troublesome was the juxtaposition of rapid decline with large population, especially as it became clear that this alarming trajectory was not unique. By the end of the nineteenth century, the North American passenger pigeon, which had been estimated to number in the billions, was extinct in the wild. The fate of the North American bison, whose population had included as many as thirty million, depended on a mere handful of individuals. The U. S. Congress established Yellowstone National Park in 1872, at least in part to protect the bison. Across the British Empire, inspired by a mixture of conservationist feeling and the desire to ensure the continued availability of wild animals to shoot, game laws were enacted to protect designated species. These measures limited the number, age, and sex of animals that could be shot; the season for hunting; and, in some places, who was eligible to apply for licenses. (Large carnivores, considered to be competitors of human hunters, were universally excluded from protection). In 1900, Britain hosted a conference for representatives of European nations with colonies in sub-Saharan Africa. It resulted in the Convention for the Preservation of Wild Animals, Birds and Fish, which they all signed. Subsequent official British grumbling, however, suggested that it may not have been followed by much action on the part of some signatories. In 1903, a group of distinguished British zoologists, colonial officials, and sportsmen founded the Society for Preservation of the Wild Fauna of the Empire. After several rechristenings, the society continues to thrive as Fauna and Flora International; its succession of names reflects the changing politics of conservation during the twentieth century.

These institutional initiatives came too late for the quagga, as they did in North America for the passenger pigeon, though not for the bison. But there has always been some question about whether rumors of the quagga's disappearance had been exaggerated. Unsurprisingly, in view of their similarity to the plains zebra, sightings were occasionally reported. Formal and informal nomenclature also contributed to this protracted uncertainty. Vernacular terms tended not to distinguish between the quagga and its closest relative. Afrikaner farmers and sportsmen referred to both quaggas and the persistently numerous plains zebras as "quagga." This allegedly onomatopoetic word echoed the sound made by the animals themselves and was borrowed from a local African language. When Theodore Roosevelt visited the Cape Colony in 1909, he used "quagga" in this sense. He found the animals beautiful and said that he "never molested them save to procure specimens for the museums, or food for the porters, who like their rather rank flesh." So he only shot about twenty of them.

The Scottish zoologist William Cossar Ewart offered a more concrete illustration of their perceived interchangeability a few years earlier. He was concerned that, indifferent to advances in the biology of mammalian reproduction, stockbreeders clung to the theory of telegony: the notion that the father of a female animal's first child was also in some sense the father of any subsequent offspring. The main evidence adduced in support of this idea was a series of foals produced much earlier in the century, by a mare whose first consort had been a quagga. Her later foals had been sired by ordinary horses, but they all showed more or less prominent striping on their legs, the result of atavism—reversion to an ancestral condition—rather than telegony. Ewart recruited mares of different breeds to repeat the original mare's reproductive experiences, but since there were no available quagga studs to service them, he substituted a common zebra. His experiment attracted wide appreciation, from which the replacement stallion did not detract.

When thinking taxonomically, however, most naturalists firmly differentiated the quagga and the plains zebra. Pennant had even derided some benighted colleagues who considered them a single species, with quaggas the males and zebras the females (or possibly vice versa). Systematic classification was a quintessentially metropolitan project, so taxonomists never attempted to consult the people who lived in closest proximity to the animals. Thus, the quagga was officially designated *Equus quagga* in 1784, and the plains zebra was named *Equus burchelli* in 1824. This formal distinction lasted for two centuries, but the emergence of genetic analysis suggested that their relationship was still closer—not separate species but (at most) subspecies of a single species. The rules of biological nomenclature dictate that when two previously recognized species are combined, the earlier designation takes precedence. So at least in name, all living plains zebras, along with their remains preserved in museums, have become quaggas—or at least *Equus quagga*. Depending on how the degree of difference between subspecies is evaluated, this taxonomic convergence may call extinction itself into question.

Defined in their original restricted sense, quaggas have possessed more charisma since their demise than they did when they roamed the grasslands of the southern Cape. Along with other recent extinctions, quaggas have attracted aficionados spurred by a combination of nostalgia, zoophilia, and romantic attachment to place. This same combination often motivates rewilding movements—proposals to return settled or cultivated areas to their previous nonhuman inhabitant. Advocates often argue that the reintroduction of vanished species would aid in the ecological restoration of their former habitats. Neither the discursive overlap indicated by the revised zebra nomenclature nor the molecular overlap on which it is based has persuaded quagga fans that the elusive object of their desire has been in front of them all the time. But ironically, the newly identified proximity has seemed to bring the resurrection of former difference within realistic reach. The Quagga Project was founded in South Africa in 1987. Its website describes the project as a "group of dedicated people" who wished to rectify "a tragic mistake made over a hundred years ago through greed and short-sightedness." It applies the selection techniques developed by livestock breeders. Plains zebras considered to be most quagga-like are mated, so that each succeeding generation resembles the vanished quagga more closely, at least to the human eye. As with many belated attempts to rectify past mistakes, it is hard to know whether seeing should be believing.

Suggestions for Further Reading

Fitter, Richard, and Sir Peter Scott. *The Penitent Butchers: 75 Years of Wildlife Conservation*. London: Collins, 1978.

Heywood, Peter. "The Micro-politics of Macromolecules in the Taxonomy and Restoration of Quaggas." *Kronos: Southern African Histories* 41, 1 (2015): 314–37.

Pennant, Thomas. "Quagga." In *History of Quadrupeds,* 14–15. London: White and White, 1793.

"Quagga." In *The Royal Natural History,* edited by Richard Lydekker, 2:506–7. London: London: Warne, 1894.

The Quagga Project: The Quagga Revival South Africa. Stellenbosch University. Accessed October 8, 2018. https://quaggaproject.org.

Ritvo, Harriet. "Understanding Audiences and Misunderstanding Audiences: Some Publics for Science." In *Noble Cows and Hybrid Zebras: Essays on Animals and History,* 103–22. Charlottesville: University of Virginia Press, 2010.

Roosevelt, Theodore. *African Game Trails: An Account of the African Wanderings of an American Hunter-Naturalist*. London: Murray, 1910.

Swart, Sandra. "Zombie Zoology: History and Reanimating Extinct Animals." In *The Historical Animal*, edited by Susan Nance, 54–71. Syracuse, NY: Syracuse University Press, 2015.

Q is also for . . .

Quahog
Quail
Quetzal
Quokka
Quoll

is for

RACCOON

The Animal Wall in Cardiff, Wales, is one of the city's architectural highlights. It once surrounded Cardiff Castle and is now a celebrated Bute Park attraction. Its stone merlons are topped by boldly carved animal statues representing much of the territorial range of the former British Empire. The wall features fifteen species, including three lions, a bear, hyena, pelican, anteater, beaver, and not just one, but two raccoons.

For some observers, the raccoons may seem an incongruous addition to the otherwise iconic or exotic species along the wall's expanse. They carry little of the lions' weighty symbolism (see L IS FOR LION), the lynx's

....

"Up a Tree—Colonel Bull and the Yankee 'Coon,'" by John Tenniel.
From *Punch*, January 11, 1862. Courtesy of John Hay Library, Brown University.

romantic Northern associations, or the beaver's fur trade significance. And for many of their human neighbors in the United States and Canada, raccoons are a commonplace presence, a garbage-can-raiding, attic-intruding nuisance, certainly not worthy of memorialization in stone. Yet raccoons have historically been deeply entangled with imperial economies and the expansionist ambitions of Britain and its nation-state successors of Canada and the United States. This underappreciated story illuminates much about the imperial project and its legacies.

Raccoons have been other-than-human relatives, neighbors, food, clothing, companions, and ceremonial beings to Indigenous peoples since time immemorial. They were also well known to various colonial powers during European extractive enterprises in the Americas. But the Imperial Raccoon is largely a British creation. Indeed, if any single name for the masked and ringtailed nocturnal creature was to be known the world over, it should have been a variant on the Anishinaabe *esiban*: "one who picks up things." This term was intelligible to more than a dozen other Algonquian-speaking peoples stretching from the East Coast and eastern woodlands of the continent, across the prairies, and nearly to the Pacific. Yet the name that dominates in the global imagination— *raccoon*—is the English corruption of a geographically narrow and culturally specific term. For that we can thank Captain John Smith and his excursions on behalf of the Virginia Company, made most famous through his exaggerated ceremonial interactions with a young Powhatan woman named Matoaka—better known by her nickname, Pocahontas.

In 1608, Smith published *A True Relation of Such Occurrences and Accidents of Note as Hath Hapned in Virginia*. Initially attributed to an anonymous colonist, this document chronicles the many struggles of the Jamestown settlement to that point. Smith describes his first meeting with Wahunsenecawh, principal chief of the Powhatan Confederacy in Tsenacommacah, the territory in which the colonists presumed to make their settlement. He recounts first seeing "Emperor" Wahunsenecawh— also known as Chief Powhatan—"proudly lying vppon a Bedftead a foote high vpon tenne or twelue Mattes, richly hung with manie Chaynes of great Pearles about his necke, and couered with a great Couering of Rahaughcums."

The Algonquian Powhatan word *arakunem* roughly means "one who scratches with its hands." Smith's various phonetic iterations in other writings include *Aroughcun* and *Arocoun*. By 1634, in William Woods's *New England's Prospect*, the spelling had come closer to our own—

Rackoone—and by the eighteenth century would, with few exceptions, become the *raccoon* we know today.

The Spanish certainly knew of raccoons in their colonial ventures. Naturalist Virginia C. Holmgren makes a compelling argument that Christopher Columbus wrote of them as *perro mastin*, the "clownlike dog," for their playfulness and mask-like facial pelage. She suggests that raccoons were among the cargo Columbus brought back to Spain. French fur traders and voyageurs, too, encountered the *chat sauvage* and came to know raccoons quite quickly as food, fur, and pets. Yet it is telling that our first recording in the English language focuses entirely on the raccoon's pelt and its association with the presumed wilderness and ostensibly savage inhabitants of North America. This relationship would define the raccoon's symbolism as a colonial commodity and emblem of North America. It would quickly come to be known as a distinctive symbol of the upstart United States and its own imperial influence across the world—more subtle, perhaps, but no less enduring than the bald eagle.

By the eighteenth century, raccoons were an internationally recognized symbol of both the bounty and untameability of the British North American colonies, although these associations were in increasing tension. They were not among the most prized quarry in the fur trade, but their ubiquity made them a dependable source of income for the Hudson's Bay Company and the North West Trading Company, as well as with independent fur traders farther to the south. And because they were a common and easy fur source for settlers and Indigenous peoples, they became associated with a particular kind of masculine colonial frontier wildness—and, less positively, with a backward, ill-educated, uncouth lifestyle.

As relations between the British Crown and the colonies that would become the United States cooled and then shattered, the raccoon took on a dual significance. To more revolution-minded colonists, they embodied a kind of nervy pluck and determination born of an undomesticated land, inflected by ideas of the noble savage popular with French Enlightenment thinkers. To elite colonial Tories and overseas Crown authorities (who were deeply suspicious of French intellectual and colonial influence), they reflected the cultural and political degradation of backwoods savages and their debauched Continental allies. Loyal subjects in Canada were increasingly associated with the hard-working, dependable beaver and the elite hats made from its luxurious pelt. But raccoons—in the form of frontiersmen's rough-and-ready coonskin caps—were increasingly seen as humble symbols of rebel patriotism, rooted in an untamed and untameable land. Thus, the iconic coonskin cap made its leap from practical fashion accessory to revolutionary and national symbol, detached from but still intersecting with British imperialism, especially as it related to the United States.

Raccoons became inextricably associated with American political identity and commercial expansionism in the years following the Revolution. Yet this association was far more about the ideal in the popular imagination than the reality. The celebrities most firmly associated with raccoon fur and the American frontier had rather less interest in them than did their contemporaries and descendants. Davy Crockett may have worn a coonskin hunting cap during his service in the anti-British War of 1812, but later in his political life, he seems to have used it primarily as a way of affirming his backwoods authenticity to Tennessee voters. Contrary to Hollywood depictions, Crockett likely did not wear such a cap when he died at the Alamo in 1836. Kentucky frontiersman, American expansionist, and virulent Indian killer Daniel Boone was often associated with the iconic coonskin cap in popular depictions of his time but, according to his son, he hated wearing them. (The coonskin association of Crockett and Boone that circulated in their own lifetimes was cemented in the twentieth century by Fess Parker's television portrayals of both men wearing the same cap, a pop-culture phenomenon that found great popularity in Britain and across the Commonwealth.) As official representative of the fledgling United States to France in the early years during the Revolutionary War, Benjamin Franklin played shrewdly on French stereotypes about the dignity of the "natural man." Forgoing a powdered wig and elaborate court dress, he wore a shapeless fur hat and simple, homespun clothing. But contrary to the still-popular claim that he wore a raccoon-skin hat at court, he more likely wore marten or sable fur instead (though their association with class privilege make them less appealing for this nationalist myth). The coonskin cap is so firmly linked to idealized frontier Americanism that it remains inextricably tied to the legacies of these men. Its deeper roots, however, are in the cultural and commercial interests of British imperialism.

Beyond its pelt, the raccoon as hunted quarry becomes another powerful symbol in the nineteenth century, one with a particularly gruesome human legacy. By the eighteenth century, the destruction of larger carnivores in Great Britain made the once-verminous foxes a more acceptable quarry for expressions of elite British masculinity, but large animals were still relatively common for upper-class white hunters in North America. And though the backwoods wilderness was a useful symbol during the American Revolution, it was less appealing for a young, ambitious nation-state eager to affirm its maturity and sophistication among its international peers.

The dramatic rise of urbanization, the fur trade giving way to other industries, and the impacts of significant population and habitat decline diminished the raccoon's significance as rebellious U.S. national symbol, except in the most romanticized and negative representations. Sir John Tenniel's caricature of Abraham Lincoln as a cringing raccoon, treed by Britain's John Bull, plays on the president's reputation as an unsophisticated rustic against a more astute and powerful enemy. It was a reference to the Trent Affair, a tense Civil War standoff that erupted when the U.S. Navy took Confederate diplomats from a British vessel and jailed them. Facing another possible armed conflict, Lincoln backed down and ordered the diplomats released—a widely criticized decision that gave his enemies further evidence of his unsuitability for the presidency. Tenniel's mockery of Lincoln as a fearful beast would only have added to the humiliation. And the conflation of the rustic backwoods raccoon with Lincoln's (and, by extension, America's) presumed political naïveté would have been familiar to *Punch*'s main readership.

Always an ambivalent icon, the common raccoon also came to be firmly linked with degraded rural impoverishment for the growing U.S. white middle class. In the waning days of slavery and the reactionary politics of Reconstruction and Jim Crow, it became particularly tied to racist white caricatures of rural African Americans. As a reference to humans, "coon" had originally been a slightly admiring term for a shrewd white rustic; it gradually encompassed the white minstrel character of Zip Coon, a racist stereotype that mocked Black dandies as having social (and economic) ambition beyond their natural capacity. The violently anti-Black "coon" epithet synthesizes these currents around the time of Henry Clay's unsuccessful 1844 presidential run for the Whig Party. He proudly wore the label "the Old Kentucky Coon," playing on his humble roots and reputation as an able politician. But his vocal opposition to the annexation of Texas as a slaveholding state helped his Democratic opponents portray the slave-owning Clay as supporting an antislavery platform. These accusations helped erode support in the South. With Clay's subsequent election loss, the negative association between "coon," Zip Coon, and African Americans was firmly established. It took little to shift white interpretations of the raccoon. It went from shrewd to sneaky and subtle to lazy, and its innate nocturnal scavenging became illicit behavior. In the mainstream white imagination of the late nineteenth century, "coon" had joined "darky" as a common epithet for African Americans, and raccoon-hunting was increasingly represented as a primarily (though not exclusively) Black activity. An entire literature of appalling dialect poetry, prose, and minstrel plays arose depicting slow, dull-witted, even degenerate Black men wasting time in brutish pleasures and avoiding respectable labor at night to chase after raccoons and other vermin in wild swamps and trackless forests.

By the early twentieth century, the term "coon hunt" took on an even more gruesome association, especially after the rise of the Ku Klux Klan: it became a common euphemism for lynching. The image of the treed and terrified raccoon surrounded by hounds and armed hunters with torches was easily read into popular photographs of brutalized Black bodies hanging from trees. Postcards depicting lynchings bore titles that not infrequently referred to coon-hunting. This was another export of U.S. cultural imperialism that found favor across the Anglosphere Commonwealth. Although raccoons are not indigenous to either Australia or South Africa, "coon" has long been used as a white racial slur against the Indigenous peoples of both countries.

As symbols and as living animals, raccoons continue to confound their human neighbors. They are smart, adaptable, and notoriously disinterested in human presumptions of property. Their curiosity and relative fearlessness around humans make them less easily dominated than most wild animals. Thus, they are more likely to take advantage of human-built environments and their resources. Introduced into Europe from North America in the mid-twentieth century, raccoons predictably escaped from captivity in short order. With most potential predator species diminished or destroyed long before their arrival, raccoon populations grew robust. In Germany and Spain, they are now widely considered a major invasive threat to crops, houses, and livelihoods—and British wildlife authorities nervously watch their territorial expansion. Raccoon kits were brought to Japan after the popular children's television cartoon *Araiguma Rasukaru* (*Rascal the Raccoon*) aired in 1977; they turned out to be far less adorable and more troublesome pets than anticipated once they reached sexual maturity. They were released into the wild, and like their European counterparts found a predator-free habitat conducive to explosive population growth. Widely regarded as a menace to farmers and to centuries-old architecture in many prefectures, raccoons have long been pest-control targets. Yet they remain largely undeterred in their expansion across Japan.

Even in North America, raccoons have come back from their extensive population and habitat losses of the nineteenth and early twentieth centuries. They are thriving, especially (and perhaps surprisingly) in bustling urban spaces. Raccoons are now a fixture of modern city life, admired and reviled in equal measure. They successfully navigate the complexities, dangers, and opportunities of human environments and actions in ways few other species have managed. Raccoons are survivors, like the Indigenous peoples in whose languages, relations, and ceremonies they continue to be meaningful participants. They belong to this land and to this time, as they always have. Whatever the future holds for our current imperial age, raccoons are very likely to survive it.

Suggestions for Further Reading

Bateman, P. W., and P. A. Fleming. "Big City Life: Carnivores in Urban Environments." *Journal of Zoology* 287 (2012): 1–23.

Fischman, Lisa Anne. "Coonskin Fever: Frontier Adventures in Postwar American Culture." PhD diss., University of Minnesota, 1996.

Holmgren, Virginia C. *Raccoons in History, Folklore, and Today's Backyards*. Santa Barbara, CA: Capra, 1990.

Ikeda, Tohru, Makoto Asano, Yohei Matoba, and Go Abe. "Present Status of Invasive Alien Raccoon and its Impact in Japan." *Global Environmental Research* 8, 2 (2004): 125–31.

MacClintock, Dorcas. *A Natural History of Raccoons*. Caldwell, NJ: Blackburn, 2002.

Roediger, David R. *The Wages of Whiteness: Race and the Making of the American Working Class*. New York: Verso, 1991.

Schroeder, Patricia. "Passing for Black: Coon Songs and the Performance of Race." *Journal of American Culture* 33, 2 (2010): 139–53.

Seton, Ernest Thompson. *Life-Histories of Northern Animals*. New York: Scribner's, 1909.

Smith, John. *The Generall Historie of Virginia, New-England and the Summer Isles*. London: Sparkes, 1624.

Zeveloff, Samuel I. *Raccoons: A Natural History*. Washington, DC: Smithsonian Institution, 2002.

R is also for . . .

Raccoon-kin ringtail
Rat
Rattlesnake
Raven
Rhinoceros

is for

SCORPION

STAMPING IT OUT.

A painful necessity both for John Bull and for the Afghan Scorpion.

T he scorpion, with its notoriously painful and sometimes
deadly sting, was a recurrent figure in the modern British imperial imagination. Travelers from the Caribbean to the Cape
recorded encounters with the creature, variously categorizing it as an
insect, a reptile, or one of the many "prowling beasts of prey" faced by
colonial settlers and sojourners. Medical men were preoccupied with
antivenomous cures, as so many victims of the scorpion's bite came to
them seeking an antidote. Missionary wives were the most likely to
name the scorpion as an impediment to feeling at home in the empire:
wherever Christian converts were to be had, scorpions were a common

....

"Stamping It Out," by John Gordon Thomson. From *Fun*, August 11, 1880.

Courtesy of Bodleian Library.

feature of household life. Scorpions were not simply underfoot; they were to be found everywhere, waiting to inflict poison on their unsuspecting prey. Scorpions skulked behind doors, crept into pillow shams, and crawled into the folds of petticoats. They even climbed up the pajama sleeves of colonizers who dreamed of dominion, perhaps, but whose peaceful sleep was interrupted by visions of the many treacherous creatures lurking beneath their beds.

The scorpion was, and is, a zodiac sign. It was also a common name for British ships. The scorpion sting was a powerful metaphor for betrayal: the kind that creeps up on a person and strikes without remorse, wounding (if not killing) the lover, the sovereign, the trusting friend. The "scorpion-lash" appears all over English fiction in the age of empire. In women's writing about lovers' quarrels, the "scorpion in the bosom" often signified the ultimate violation. Its sting delivered the intimate bedchamber wound, a pricking that foretells the lingering pain and heartbreak yet to come.

The scorpion, of course, was also real, and its sting was the precursor to considerable physical torment and even death. Tourists warned that scorpions were legion: they came up out of floorboards and might even be found in the pages of a book. Anticipation of the scorpion's deadly presence was considered a sign of long and wise colonial experience. Its deadliness was even a pretext for white settlement: according to a report from New South Wales, "owing to their prolific powers, [the scorpions'] extirpation cannot be effected, at least while the country remains uncleared." The scorpion was also an evangelical cautionary tale. Missionary magazines, especially those written for children, often used the story of a scorpion's sting as evidence of God's intentions, whether the victim lived or died. If they were spared, it was taken as a sign that the heavens protected Christians and their civilizing mission in the empire. Meanwhile, "death by scorpion bite" was both an eye-catching headline and a warning of what believers were prepared to sacrifice for Christ.

Colonial writers were not apologetic about killing scorpions, in part because they felt licensed to do so by the New Testament. Luke 10:19 reads, "Behold, I give unto you power to tread on serpents and scorpions, and over all the power of the enemy: and nothing shall by any means hurt you." The leap from scriptural authority to a mandate over all imperial creatures was not hard to make.

Women were no less averse to killing scorpions than men. For some missionary wives, it was a point of pride, evidence of the link between a clean mission home and other forms of mastery. It could also shed light on cultural difference with an evangelical purpose. In the *Wesleyan Juvenile Offering*, one woman reported that she had given her shoe to a servant to fend off a scorpion that was attacking a "heathen" child in the middle of a Mohurram celebration. She concluded by underscoring how calm and quiet Christian services were in contrast. And according to the *Illustrated Missionary News*, the Reverend J. L. Wyatt had reported that Indian mothers were known to tell girls that if they touched Christians, they would suffer the symptoms of a scorpion sting.

Colonial observers took satisfaction in the fact that, by all accounts, Natives were just as fearful of the scorpion as they were. Botanists and doctors (some of them medical missionaries) tallied the number of stings and deaths per year as part of their recordkeeping, noting that local people often came to them for cures when homegrown remedies failed. This was taken as evidence of Native superstition, in implicit contrast to Christians' confident mandate to crush them underfoot. Victorian periodical literature is teeming with species lists and other forms of inventory that note vernacular names for the scorpion in different regions. There are also local axioms about the scorpion and its power, from the Pashtun battle saying "Wise men do not kill the scorpion and leave his brood" to the attitude of the nonviolent high-caste Hindu who "will not kill a snake or a scorpion, though he will desire another to do so." This catalogue of scorpion bites, cures, and sightings was matched by a fascination with "scorpion-grass"—the "forget-me-not" by any other name.

Because of their potentially deadly stings, scorpions were feared and even loathed. They were also seen as "enemies," "combatants" and in some contexts, instruments of war. Considered "pugnacious" as well as dangerous, scorpions had a history of connection to battle in South Asia. The research of the East India Company historian Sir Henry Elliot supported arguments that scorpions were used as "early Asiatic fire weapons"—either in conjunction with bituminous materials or literally as airborne insect-missiles themselves. In an essay for the *Journal of the Asiatic Society of Bengal*, Major General R. Maclagan entertained the possibility that calling such missiles scorpions was simply metaphorical. But he did not dismiss the possibility that some hybrid form of the creature had indeed been weaponized, especially as the region in question was well known for both coal deposits and scorpion populations.

The metaphorical possibilities of the scorpion as an agent of anticolonial struggle were highly political in Victoria's empire. Daniel O'Connell, the Irish radical reformer and early anticolonial politician, lobbed a rhetorical grenade at Edward Smith Stanley, Lord Derby: during rancorous political debates about the Irish question in 1840, he called him "Scorpion Stanley" for his anti-Catholic attitudes. The nickname stuck to Stanley well into the 1850s; it was invoked to suggest his willingness to rile up "the wild rage of the Protestant rabble of England," as the *Bengal Catholic Herald* put it. It was also turned back on O'Connell, of whom *Figaro in London* said, "There are many animals whose sting lies entirely in their tails, and O'Connell is one of them."

An image from the Second Anglo-Afghan War reflects a wide-reaching cultural dialogue about the challenges that the colonial creature world posed to British imperial ambition. The scorpion is pictured as a menacing, hybrid thing. Half insect, half Afghan tribal fighter, it scurries underfoot and seems to evade the attempts of John Bull (wearing a pith helmet) to stamp it out. If Britain has the backing of scripture, an enemy combatant that exceeds human boundaries and must be exterminated tests the capacity of the British soldier to win the battle definitively. In this illustration, nature is hybridized and weaponized, threatening the traditional military campaign with insect guerilla warfare. The geopolitics of this contest is highly gendered, and not just in terms of manly English men seeking to annihilate half-breeds. Look carefully in the corner and you will see India, which was often represented as female in the nineteenth century. Here she evokes the Queen, who had been made Empress of India by act of parliament in 1876.

The stakes of winning in Afghanistan were very high: not only did India have to be protected; the vulnerability of all of Victoria's empire must be defended. British military success is not enough—there must also be species domination. The scorpion might well remind Victorian readers of the precariousness of the line between the human and the insect form. In scientific terms, this was also the case. "Stamping it Out" was a political cartoon, designed to represent the stakes of boundary-crossing along the Northwest frontier and to dramatize the limits and possibilities of Britain's territorial claims there. The "Afghan scorpion" was a convenient biopolitical symbol; but it would not have been the only one seen by readers who followed imperial events and officials in the press. *Punch* and other political humorists routinely turned contemporary figures into hybrid creatures. One artist rendered Winston

Churchill part man, part caterpillar in its larval stage—an attempt to send up the 1902 Balfour government via a satire on *Alice in Wonderland*. (See also A IS FOR APE, especially the Darwin image; R IS FOR RACCOON, the Lincoln image.)

As for the scorpion, late Victorian commentators exhibited tremendous interest in its historical and contemporary forms precisely because it was not just bimodal (half-crustacean) but antimodal (neither reptile nor insect). According to Allen Charles Grant Blairfindie, it was considered "neither fish nor fowl, nor good red herring" or "a spider-kind, though not a thoroughgoing spider." That indeterminacy challenged easy forms of classification inside the animal kingdom. It also blurred the line that safeguarded evolutionary hierarchy and species difference across the human/nonhuman divide. Whether through the seriousness of scientific investigation, the evangelical concern of the missionary in the field, or the satiric wit of the political commentator, the scorpion was a commonplace colonial menace that brought all kinds of danger to the doorstep. And the "Afghan scorpion" is a rather arresting visual trace of how such species confusion might be used to throw the British soldier off-balance, conjuring that Pashtun saying about the wise man who should kill both the scorpion *and* his "brood"—if he can.

Suggestions for Further Reading

Blairfindie, Allen Charles Grant (attributed). "The Modest Scorpion." *Cornhill Magazine* 21 (1893): 643–54.

Brendon, Piers. *Churchill's Bestiary: His Life through Animals*. London: O'Meara, 2018.

Freedgood, Elaine. *Victorian Writing about Risk: Imagining a Safe England in a Dangerous World*. Cambridge, UK: Cambridge University Press, 2006.

Justice, Austin R., Artur Stasiek, and Archana Upadhyay. "Stamping It Out (1880): Imagining the Second Anglo-Afghan War." *SourceLab* 1, no. 3 (2018). https://doi.org/10.21900/j.sourcelab.v1.442.

Maclagan, Major General R. "On Early Asiatic Fire-Weapons." *Journal of the Asiatic Society of Bengal* 45, 1 (1876): 30–71.

"O'Connell and His Tail." *Figaro in London*, September 1, 1838, 135.

"The Proclamation." *Bengal Catholic Herald*, November 6, 1852, 630.

Wyatt, Rev. J. L. "Zenana Work." *The Mission Field*, September 1, 1886, 276.

S is also for . . .

Sheep
Shrew
Sloth
Squirrel

is for

TIGER

For the British, the tiger personified the wildness and danger of the alien environments that they encountered in South and Southeast Asia. A stealthy, elusive, powerful creature, the tiger inspired a mixture of awe and terror because of its swift, deadly attacks on prey. To "ride the tiger" is an idiomatic expression that describes the futility of controlling the uncontrollable. It is an apt metaphor for the challenges that confronted the British as they struggled to impose and maintain imperial control over the peoples of India and neighboring territories.

. . . .

Lord Curzon, Viceroy of India, and his wife, Lady Mary Curzon,
after a successful tiger hunt, Hyderabad, India, 1903.

For the Indian regimes that the British overthrew, the tiger played an important role in royal recreation and symbolism. The Mughal emperors exhibited their martial skills and mastery over nature by conducting carefully choreographed tiger hunts. Shah Jehangir is reputed to have killed eighty tigers during his reign. The Nawab of Awadh, a semiautonomous state in north India, entertained visiting British dignitaries with fights between tigers, buffaloes, and bears in enclosed pits. For Tipu Sultan, ruler of the kingdom of Mysore in south-central India, the tiger was the official symbol of his reign, an emblem of power emblazoned on his throne, his soldiers' livery, and even the mouths of his cannon. His craftsmen also produced Tipu's Tiger, a striking life-sized wooden sculpture of a tiger mauling a British soldier, its ingeniously mechanized inner workings emitting sounds of the tiger's grunts and the soldier's screams. It was meant to celebrate Tipu's victories against the British in the first and second Anglo-Mysore wars. The tide turned in the third war, with the British conquering Mysore and killing Tipu in 1799. Tipu's Tiger became a war trophy. It was shipped to London and put on display, becoming a hugely popular attraction at the East India Office and then the Victoria and Albert Museum, where it remains. No single object did more to associate India with the fierce and deadly tiger in the minds of the British public.

This association was reinforced by regular reports of tiger attacks on Britons in India, Ceylon, Malaya, and elsewhere across South and Southeast Asia. One of the first cases to attract widespread attention in Britain was the death of Lt. Hugh Munro, son of General Sir Hector Munro, who was mauled by a tiger during a picnic near Calcutta in 1792. Whether it inspired William Blake to pen his famous lines—"Tyger Tyger, burning bright, In the forest of the night"—two years after the incident, it is impossible to say; but the poem certainly evoked the tiger's fearsome reputation. The public memory of Munro's death would remain alive for decades to come. A popular figurine produced by Staffordshire pottery works from the 1810s to the 1830s portrayed the young officer in the tiger's jaws, with the positioning of the pair strikingly similar to Tipu's Tiger. Stories of Britons attacked by tigers appeared repeatedly in British newspapers during the nineteenth century. Typical headlines included "An Officer Killed by a Tiger," "Encounter with a Man-Eating Tiger," and "Fatal Tiger Hunt in India."

Most of the victims of these attacks met their fate while hunting. For the British who ruled India and neighboring territories, few recreational activities surpassed shooting wild and exotic game, and none held greater prestige than the tiger hunt. Given the dangers the tiger posed for hunters—not to mention their beaters and guides, though the risks to these local people rarely received notice—a successful hunt was regarded as the supreme test of masculinity. Breathless tales of tiger hunts featured in colonial memoirs and books about hunting adventures (one of the most popular genres of the nineteenth century). Tiger skins and heads were displayed on the floors and walls of Indian bungalows and English country houses, physical reminders of these feats of manly courage.

The tiger also assumed increasing symbolic significance for the imperial project itself. It represented the pitiless savagery that the British associated with the Indian rebellion of 1857–58 and other violent protests against their self-supposed benevolent rule. One of the starkest expressions of this association was John Tenniel's famous 1857 cartoon "The British Lion's Vengeance on the Bengal Tiger," which appeared in *Punch* in response to the news that over one hundred British women and children had been killed at Cawnpore by Indian rebels (see L IS FOR LION). The cartoon shows the British lion leaping on an Indian tiger that looms over the prone, presumably dead bodies of a white woman and child. The clear message was that Britain would avenge this heinous crime. Other illustrations and paintings of this era made similar use of the tiger to evoke the savage nature of the Indigenous society that the British struggled to govern.

By the late nineteenth century, however, the fear of rebellion had subsided. Tiger hunts had turned into what historian William Storey had termed "pageants of colonial power." Viceroys and other leading colonial officials enthusiastically adopted the Mughal tradition of shooting tigers from *howdahs* on the backs of elephants. This was the most expensive, luxurious, and risk-free way of hunting the dangerous beasts. Its stately trappings and army of attendants gave it a ceremonial splendor that heralded the grandeur of empire. Anglo-Indians came to refer to it as the "sport of princes." Not surprisingly, authorities arranged these extravaganzas for the various members of the royal family who toured India frequently after 1870. The Prince of Wales, the Duke of Edinburgh, and other royal luminaries experienced the thrill of tiger hunts on the backs of elephants, and great efforts were made to ensure that each of them bagged a trophy. No one, however, relished shooting tigers for sport more than Lord Curzon, Viceroy of India from 1899 to 1905. He went on numerous tiger hunts during his years in India and carefully documented his triumphs in photographs. In one example, he stands with the slain tiger at his feet—the personification of imperial masculinity. The message is reinforced both by his wife's presence at his side and by the absence of any Indians. An impresario of imperial symbolism, Curzon understood that this photograph would be read as a sign of Britain's mastery over India itself.

While the tiger continued to be characterized as the most dangerous creature to inhabit the jungles of South Asia, the danger it presented was increasingly transposed onto Indian subjects in the British imagination. There was nothing new about tiger attacks on the poor peasants, herdsmen, and other Native peoples; their struggles to make a living required them to encroach on the animal's natural habitat. By the turn of the century, however, the perils that "man-eating" tigers posed to villagers had intruded into the consciousness of British tiger hunters and those who followed their exploits. Ridding rural communities of the tigers that terrorized them allowed hunters to cast this blood sport as a humanitarian endeavor and connect it to the paternalistic rationale for imperial rule. The most famous hunter to defend his actions in these altruistic terms was Jim Corbett, who killed a large number of tigers and leopards during his career. In the bestselling *Man-Eaters of Kumaon* and other books, he portrayed his exploits as benevolent responses to desperate pleas from defenseless villagers. At a time when nationalists were challenging the moral foundations of empire, British readers found reassurance in this variation on the imperial theme of the "white man's burden."

Corbett also campaigned for the creation of an Indian national reserve to protect the tiger, which had become endangered as a result of overhunting by people like himself. This change of heart reflected a broader conservation effort by the late imperial state. Measures were enacted to protect natural habitats and their native wildlife from the depredations of humans. These policies were not targeted at British hunters, who were recast as custodians of nature. They were meant for the Indians who used these lands to collect firewood, graze animals, and provide other essential resources for their families: such activities now were deemed criminal. By the 1920s, the coerciveness of these measures sparked peasant protests, which soon fed into the wider political unrest of the era. The British learned that even the seemingly wild and remote regions where tigers roamed were not immune to nationalist agitation.

The tiger became a source of inspiration for nationalists. Hindu nationalist iconography included images of Durga, the goddess of war, riding a tiger—a feat no mortal could match. After independence, the India government proclaimed the tiger its national animal. Bangladesh and Malaysia did the same. They have brought us full circle, investing the tiger with much the same symbolic meaning as an emblem of state power that it held for Tipu Sultan and other rulers across the region prior to British imperial conquest.

Still, the symbolic importance of the tiger to some of the countries it inhabits has done little to safeguard it. The number of tigers has declined from an estimated one hundred thousand at the start of the twentieth century to less than four thousand today. Three species are already extinct; several others are classified as critically endangered. The Indian government has responded to this threat in recent decades by establishing some two dozen tiger reserves around the country. This has helped to ensure that the Bengal tiger, currently numbering some 2,500, is by far the most plentiful tiger species. But poaching, the loss of habitat, and clashes with villagers put the tiger's survival at continued risk. These problems are even more pronounced in Malaysia, Sumatra, and other parts of Southeast Asia. The 1981 Convention on International Trade in Endangered Species has done little to diminish the illicit trade in tiger bone, blood, and other body parts, which are highly prized for their medicinal benefits, especially by the Chinese. The combination of economic and environmental pressures raises the question of whether the wild tiger can be saved.

Suggestions for Further Reading

Booth, Martin. *Carpet Sahib: A Life of Jim Corbett*. Delhi: Oxford University Press, 1990.

Crane, Ralph, and Lisa Fletcher. "Picturing the Indian Tiger: Imperial Iconography in the Nineteenth Century." *Victorian Literature and Culture* 42, 3 (2014): 369–86.

Dinerstein, Eric, Coulby Loucks, Eric Wikranamaye, Joshua Ginsberg, Eric Sanderson, John Seidensticker, and Jessica Forrest, et. al. "The Fate of Wild Tigers." *BioScience* 57, 6 (2007): 508–14.

Guynup, Sharon. "A Concise History of Tiger Hunting in India." *National Geographic Society Newsroom*, March 10, 2014. https://blog.nation algeographic.org/2014/03/10/a-concise-history-of-tiger-hunting-in -india/.

MacKenzie, John M. *The Empire of Nature: Hunting, Conservation, and British Imperialism*. Manchester: Manchester University Press, 1988.

Sramek, Joseph. "'Face Him Like a Tiger': Tiger Hunting, Imperialism, and British Masculinity in Colonial India, 1800–1875." *Victorian Studies* 48, 4 (2006): 659–80.

Storey, William K. "Big Cats and Imperialism: Lion and Tiger Hunting in Kenya and Northern India, 1898–1930." *Journal of World History* 2, 2 (1991): 135–73.

Stronge, Susan. *Tipu's Tigers*. London: Victoria and Albert Museum, 2009.

Thapar, Valmik. *The Illustrated Tigers of India*. New Delhi: Oxford University Press, 2007.

T is also for . . .

Tasmanian devil
Termite
Tortoise

is for

UNICORN

George Orwell's famed 1941 essay, *The Lion and the Unicorn: Socialism and the English Genius*, which pleads for an appropriately socialist English revolution in the face of Nazi Germany, never actually mentions the unicorn after the title page. The status of the lion and unicorn as emblems of the British national self barely needed qualification (see L IS FOR LION). Most British national symbols are inherently also imperial ones, as many of the chapters in this volume suggest. Orwell was no stranger to this truth. For example, the "English revolution" he called for could succeed only if "we tell the Indians they are free to secede if they want to." For him, the promise of equality between Britain and India, Burma, Malaya, and all the African colonies was coeval with the nationalization of industry and agriculture and "abolishing the autonomy of public schools and the older universities" in Britain. Even radical dreams of populist social democracy failed to escape the pervasive sway of imperial symbols like the unicorn.

The unicorn was a ubiquitous sign of British imperial dominion. With the dynastic Union of the Crowns in 1603 that led to the nomination of James I as the single monarch of England, Ireland, and Scotland, the

....

The coat of arms of Great Britain. Used by permission of Getty Images, object number: LS006924.

unicorn came to proudly symbolize the Scottish claim to distinction from and equality with England. Originating in Scottish royal heraldry, it subsequently joined the lion on the British royal coat of arms, hailing the onset of greater Scottish participation in plantation oversight in Ireland and colonization in the Americas in the seventeenth century. In Scotland itself, the unicorn has been considered a "national" animal since the fourteenth century. Timeworn tales of the unicorn's enmity with the English lion, its magical ability to purify anything it touches, and its unyielding strength, all of which are famously allegorized around Elizabeth I in Edmund Spenser's *The Faerie Queen* (1590), have long been a part of Scottish popular culture.

In the hands of Renaissance artists like German painter Lucas Cranach, it has also embodied Edenic innocence. Its flowing white form symbolized Christian themes of chastity and loyalty (especially to the Virgin Mary) across European miniature art, tapestries, and portraits in the sixteenth century. Through colonial missionaries, references to the unicorn in various books of the Bible made their way into catechisms across distant mission stations. The European fascination with the unicorn dates to Aristotle and Ctesias's curiosity about one-horned quadrupeds in Persia and India in the fourth century BCE. Mediterranean and Persian Islamic art featured motifs of one-horned quadruped like the *karkadann*, likely from literary descriptions of the one-horned Indian rhinoceros. These creatures symbolized monstrous strength, evidenced by the horn's ability to deftly impale or cleave and subsequently swing the assailed opponent upward into the air. Depicting monstrosity also entailed painting hybrid one-horned creatures with wings, claws, or elephantine dimensions. These served to throw into relief the relative strength of human figures—like Turkish or Mughal kings—who were portrayed in manuscripts and miniatures having subdued the monster. Greater familiarity in Europe with existing horned species such as the Arabian oryx and the African or Indian rhinoceros, however, did little to quell the unicorn's mystique. In fact, nineteenth-century English science writers often made evolutionist historical claims over the unicorn's deep past, emboldened by greater knowledge of the Arctic monodon, the narwhal.

The narwhal, lazily called the unicorn of the sea, had paralleled English unicorn myths since the sixteenth century. The English privateer Martin Frobisher, on finding a dead narwhal washed ashore on Baffin Island in 1577, tested the "sea Unicorne" for magic in its tusk. British imperial exploration of the Arctic involved the displacement of and direct violence against Inuit peoples. Frobisher's crew, for instance, kidnapped three Inuit persons on the same voyage, who died after arriving in England. By the nineteenth century, it was common for Arctic expeditions and whaling voyages to use Inuit men or rely on their Indigenous knowledge and essential commodities on Arctic expeditions and whaling voyages. In 1819, Sir William Parry's quest for the Northwest Passage through Lancaster Sound—partly with the help of "eskimaux" canoes—brought him international acclaim. His *Journal of a Voyage for the Discovery of a North West Passage* told of crew members harpooning narwhal for purposes of both science and pleasure. By 1891, the American Navy Officer Robert Peary had traded guns, ammunition, and household utensils to the "Polar Eskimo" in exchange for a vast collection of Indigenous weapons and tools for the World's Columbian Exposition in Chicago in 1893. Narwhal tusks and skin were essential to many such tools. Despite the growing physical knowledge of the narwhal, writers in popular English periodicals, echoing tales of Elizabeth I's gem-laden narwhal tusk collection and myths of King Arthur's unicorn encounters, used this knowledge to claim a maritime evolutionary ancestry for the unicorn. Herman Melville, whose *Moby-Dick* described the physiology of the "narwhale" in much detail, scoffed at the illustration of a narwhal in the 1807 London edition of the popular publication *Goldsmith's Animated Nature*: "one glimpse of which was enough to amaze one, that in this nineteenth century, such a hippogriff could be palmed for genuine upon any intelligent public of schoolboys." Colonial scientific knowledge of the narwhal did not necessarily undermine the continued mythification of the unicorn in British media. Instead, it reconstituted the mythology of the unicorn through colonial nautical allegories.

Colonialism was fundamental to reproducing the ubiquity of the fabled unicorn. In August 1829, London's popular two-penny periodical *The Mirror of Literature, Amusement, and Instruction* playfully hailed the presence of the unicorn "for ages, gallantly climbing the slippery heights of the kingly crown on show boards, carriages, transparencies, theatres, and the new matchless hydropyric, or, the fiery and watery fairy palace of Vauxhall." From nineteenth-century Vauxhall's pleasure gardens to "the gilt *confitures* of Bartholomew Fair" at Aldersgate, the writer noted, "all the dilettanti were immersed in the great national question of its shape and features." True to form, the piece then satirized the exploits of said dilettantes, many of whom were well-known colonists. One Mr. Barrow (presumably Sir John Barrow) "believed he saw it but doubted its existence" after journeying merely "three miles beyond the Cape;" one Vaillant (likely French naturalist Francois Levaillant) apparently never saw a unicorn but believed it existed "as if it had slept in his bosom and been unto him as a daughter"; and one Mr. Russell "owned a unicorn, milking it twice a day, and drove it to meet the Queen of Madagascar." The piece lampooned the fascination of Londoners with the unicorn in the wider empire. The writer added that one Mr. Ruppell (presumably German naturalist Eduard Rueppell) had "after a long sojourn in the northeast of Africa" claimed that the unicorn indeed exists in "Kordofan, if anyone knows where that is" and supposedly looked as slender as a gazelle, but was really a small horse. "By the next arrival," the piece concluded, the unicorn would hopefully not "degenerate into a cow, or worse, a goat." Unicorn stories circulated as dynamic repositories of imperial claims to "discovery," fundamentally shaping the self-fashioning of ordinary citizens in the metropole.

Through its satire, the *Mirror*'s piece powerfully highlighted another reality—unicorn myths and sightings were an extremely popular everyday vehicle for ordinary Britons to consume their empire. In particular, the association between unicorn sightings and Central Asian or African frontier outposts, such as Kordofan in Sudan, fused the fascination for mythic beast and exotic empire. This enabled greater familiarity with places outside known colonial port cities. The frequent publication of unicorn stories from abroad, in fact, mirrored the commonplace presence of unicorn imagery in other media, such as theatrical plays and public buildings. For instance, in February 1821, the *Weekly Entertainer and West of England Miscellany*, published from Sherborne in Dorset, printed a genuinely hopeful article titled "A Real Unicorn," based on communication from Major Barre Latter. Latter was in command of the kingdom of Sikkim after the 1814–16 East India Company offensive against Nepal had enabled British expansion in the northern Bengal frontier. He had apparently discovered a Tibetan manuscript confirming the unicorn's existence. The "Native" who shared the manuscript, the article claimed, described to Latter a "fierce and extremely wild" animal almost identical to "the fera Monoceros described by Pliny." Such was the debate over unicorn sightings in local periodicals that the prominent Scottish colonist and doctor, William Balfour Baikie, weighed in against rising unicorn skepticism from his settlement in Bida, then capital of the Nupe Kingdom in the Niger basin. In August 1862, London's popular science publication *The Athenaeum* carried his account "from the countries which this supposed fabulous creature is believed to inhabit." With a tone of near-definite authenticity, he listed eight names of the unicorn in languages like Fulani, Yoruba, and Hausa. He recounted how a unicorn-like animal was common in all the African kingdoms he had crossed in his voyage up the Niger, thus leaving little room for doubt. Citing news of skeletons and unicorn bones he had yet to see himself, he gravely cautioned readers that the unicorn's "non-existence is not yet proven." For the Briton abroad, pursuing the unicorn inspired a relentless suspension of disbelief, making the unicorn a constant and enticing companion.

As the nineteenth century drew to a close, the hunt to sight the unicorn led some to hazard newer origin myths. Its presence in the heraldic menagerie, one writer argued in the *London Journal* in March 1899, was rooted in the encounter between English crusaders "on the shores of Syria and Palestine" and antelopes with long straight horns that blended into one when viewed in profile. At once a mystical Oriental beast and fabled European symbol, the unicorn's fluid passage between geographies, literatures, and genres needed to be disciplined and fixed through the heroic yet erroneous British hero. Subduing the unicorn was the most definitive feature of its British representations. The unicorn on the royal coat of arms is thus always fettered, unlike its freely roaring counterpart. In the *English Review* in March 1927, one Morris Marples recounted a common Mother Goose rhyme: "The lion and the unicorn were fighting for the crown; the lion beat the unicorn and sent him out of town." While the ditty underscored a peculiarly English passion for a victorious lion, it also showed the obvious limits of prowess among the heraldic animals. The unicorn, here gendered masculine, was often historically depicted to be in need of taming. Its medieval European connotation of wildness and primitive Orientalist vigor required either the gentle touch of the mother of Christ for some artists, or the virile strength of the Scotsman per Celtic lore. By the early twentieth century, however, the chained unicorn upon flags, military buildings, currency notes, and passports, affirmed masculine British prowess more generally.

The worldly allure of the unicorn was essentially centered on its horn. Medieval European medical practices had touted unicorn horns as antidotes to poisons. This was echoed in the prolific market for horns that undergirded the European trade in healing substances. In early modern Scotland, the fear of murder by poison plagued elites and was an accessible plot device in theatre. French and Italian illustrators had been rendering the horn as magical antidote in texts like the illuminated *Bible of Borso d'Este* since the fifteenth century. In the hands of inventive apothecaries, merchants, and physicians, powdered horns—notionally of unicorns, but likely made from tusks or goat horns—coupled the animal's mythical status with physical realities. Whether by ingesting the unicorn horn in an echo of the Eucharist, or using it to make sacral or luxury objects like goblets that could nullify poisoned liquids or cure melancholy and King's Evil, Britons' physical bodies literally reconciled the unicorn's British charms with its otherwise "Oriental" provenance.

Discovering Asian uses of horns only reinforced a belief in unicorn medicine among imperial Britons. The celebrated English traveler and first female fellow elected to the Royal Geographical Society, Isabella Bird, noted this in *Unbeaten Tracks in Japan*. She recounted seeing "Dr. Nosoki's box of unicorn horns" that was "worth more than its weight in gold," which led her to pay close attention to rhinoceros horns in Chinese markets. Her contemporary, the noted Scottish heiress, travel writer, and painter, Constance F. Gordon-Cumming, described her own meeting in Osaka with a "compounder of such strange medicines as were administered to our British ancestors in the Middle Ages." Her research, she noted, was prompted by the fact that her "quaint, old, Japanese chemist of the pure and unadulterated old school" had "loyally adhered to the customs of his ancestors" against European influences emphasizing "the scientific study of medicine" in Japan. This long essay, titled "Strange Medicines" appeared in the reputed London literary magazine *The Nineteenth Century* in 1887. In it, she detailed how "the learned leeches of Europe" had, just like Eastern medicine, concluded that unicorn horns could reveal or negate poisons. Doctors in sixteenth-century Augsburg, she noted, had successfully used real unicorn horn on poisoned dogs, and "old English medical works" had found elk horn to cure epilepsy. She argued that if the "official pharmacopeia of the College of Physicians of London in 1678" could highly approve of human skulls and unicorn horn as medicines, then England also shared with Egypt, Japan, and India a history of ingesting human and animal matter that could be dated to before the Norman conquest. From spider-eating in Ireland to offering human hair to birds in Sunderland, Britain too had its strange medicines, she concluded. Invoking insidiously Orientalist views of the East as somehow truer to its antiquity than Europe, Gordon-Cumming demonstrated a singular problem of identity and difference under modern empire. Her nameless Japanese interlocutor's unchanging sameness with the past anchored her quest for an identical British antiquity. Besieged by the rapid changes of modern empire, she legitimized popular practices that bore signs of the strangeness of British pasts. These were, in her rendition, equivalent to seemingly timeless Eastern ones. Unicorns regularly spawned and bridged such perplexities of empire.

As increasing knowledge about horned quadrupeds across disparate biomes sustained unicorn myths, the appeal of the animal emerged as a peculiarly western European preoccupation. As early as December 1819, Liverpool's *The Kaleidoscope or Literary and Scientific Mirror* published a story in its miscellaneous section that read, "Mr. Bowdich, when on a mission to Ashantee inquired of the people of that country and of Dagwumba whether they had ever heard of an unicorn? Yes, replied they, 'in the white man's country.'" It is no wonder, then, that the title to Orwell's plea for an English revolution in 1941 needed no qualification.

Suggestions for Further Reading

Beer, Rüdiger Robert. *Unicorn: Myth and Reality*. New York: James Kerry, 1977.

Ettinghausen, Richard. *The Unicorn: Studies in Muslim Iconography*. Freer Gallery of Art Occasional Papers 1.3. Washington, DC: Smithsonian Institution, 1950.

Freeman, Margaret. *The Unicorn Tapestries*. New York: Metropolitan Museum of Art, 1976.

Hathaway, Nancy. *The Unicorn*. New York: Viking, 1980.

Lavers, Chris. *The Natural History of Unicorns*. New York: Harper Collins, 2009.

Mackenzie, John, and T. M. Devine, eds. *Scotland and the British Empire* (Oxford, UK: Oxford University Press, 2011).

O'Neill, Emma. "Why Is the Unicorn Scotland's National Animal? Interview with Elyse Waters." *The Scotsman*, November 19, 2015. https://www.scotsman.com/lifestyle-2-15039/why-is-the-unicorn-scotland-s-national-animal-1-3953188.

Orwell, George. *The Lion and the Unicorn: Socialism and the English Genius*. London: Secker and Warburg, 1941.

Rider, Catherine. "Medical Magic and the Church in Thirteenth-Century England." *Social History of Medicine* 24, 1. (2011): 92–107.

Rundell, Katherine. "Consider the Narwhal." *London Review of Books* 41, 3 (2019): 12.

Schoenberger, Guido. "A Goblet of Unicorn Horn." *Metropolitan Museum of Art Bulletin* 9, 10 (1951): 284–88.

Shepard, Odell. *The Lore of the Unicorn*. New York: Barnes and Noble, 1967.

U is also for . . .

Uakari monkey
Ulysses butterfly
Upupa hoopoes
Urial sheep
Umbrellabird

is for

VULTURE

V ultures have been an integral part of Parsi and Zoroastrian funeral rituals and cosmologies, shaping their notions of the passage of time and the death of the living body. Towers of silence are still found in Iran and India, where death by exposure has a long legal history. Mitra Sharafi, a scholar of Parsi legal culture under the British Empire in South Asia, has described how access to the *dakhma*, where the dead were exposed to vultures, was a key subject of legal collaboration and sanction under British rule in Bombay. Sharafi has also shown how some Parsi litigants in Secunderabad channeled British sentiments of disgust at vultures to make legal claims against the unsanitariness of burial towers. Thus, the vulture was deeply embedded in the spiritual and legal worlds of Parsi communities under empire.

Unfortunately, practices of death by exposure have also contributed to endangering several vulture species. Diclofenac, an anti-

....

"Charnel Ground, Bombay," drawing on wood by Robert Tennent, engraving by Stephen Miller and George Pearson. From John Matheson, *England to Delhi: A Narrative of Indian Travel* (London: Longmans, Green, 1870). Photo © British Library Board, HMNTS 10058.h.36./OCORW.1986.a.3018.

inflammatory chemical given to livestock, poisoned vultures feeding on their carcasses, causing a drastic decline of over 90 percent in India's vulture population between 1980 and 2010. In the January 2016 issue of *National Geographic*, Elizabeth Royte recounted how Charles Darwin found the vulture disgusting, its bald head "formed to wallow in putridity." However, in the Serengeti, vultures perform the necessary task of cleaning up carrion that would otherwise foster bacteria, insects, and diseases that could debilitate the agrarian economies of Kenya and Tanzania. The poisoning of vultures poses a tangible threat to African ecological health. Ivory poachers have often poisoned carcasses of elephants to kill off vultures whose assembly near the carcass can alert forest guards. Vulture heads, feet, and brains are also regularly used in African cultural practices and commonly sold in Durban's markets today. The international Convention on the Conservation of Migratory Species of Wild Animals now includes the creation of vulture-safe zones in India and rapid-response poisoning units in Kenya.

British doctors in the empire reluctantly admitted that vultures contributed positively to sanitation in the colonies. In 1924, the director of the London School of Hygiene and Tropical Medicine, Andrew Balfour, and his colleague Henry Scott, wrote *Health Problems of the Empire: Past, Present, and Future*. This was included in South African colonist Hugh Gunn's edited series *The British Empire: A Survey in 12 Volumes*. Scott and Balfour, comparing Jamaica and Trinidad in the West Indies to eastern India, were strongly critical of white Europeans' hygienic practices in both places. White colonists in Jamaica were particularly at fault, they wrote, for not implementing programs for general sanitation. Contrary to the opinion of Hans Sloane, they argued, that if not for the Jamaican turkey vulture (locally called the *corbeau* in Trinidad and John Crow in Jamaica), "towns in Jamaica would not be habitable." Despite the vulture's utility, the killing of vultures was historically very common across the British Empire. Vulture feathers were prized elements of women's fashion. On May 19, 1871, the *Natal Witness* advertised vulture feathers as part of a new collection of "Dunning's Imported Goods." In December 1872, the *Madras Mail* carried a similar ad by Messrs. Lewis, Milner and Co. of English House, Mount Road, "informing the ladies of Madras and Out-stations of new goods especially for the Madras season," which included vulture feathers to accompany their silks and velvets. Vulture feathers had also been part of the attire and adornments of the headgear and weapons of many east African peoples, most famously the Maasai.

Incidentally, vulture feathers were crucial to the colonial extraction of gold in southern Africa. The South African Gold-Fields Exploration Company (Limited) was formed in 1868 to capitalize on gold discoveries in northern Transvaal. Its first expedition was directed by C. J. Nelson, who had spent thirteen years in California, and commanded by Thomas Baines, an explorer fascinated by the mineral wealth of Matabeleland. In the company's charter, Baines remembered having been offered gold dust for sale by "Natives" in the Portuguese settlements on the Zambezi River. They carried the fine dust in vulture quills.

For some colonists in Africa, the vulture was an insult to be hurled at those who complicated existing ruler-subject relationships. In 1852, an angry columnist of the *D'urban Advocate* described lawyers who fought cases for African subjects in Durban's courts as "the vulture class of mortals . . . who abound most where misery, vice, and filth operate to brutalise the human race." They were supposedly taking too many cases, promoting a culture of litigation among the "Natives,'" and earning much more money than they should—all irredeemable vices to the settler capitalist or farmer. Alternatively, the vulture signified the excesses of "Native" culture. In December 1869, following a debate on whether Zulu subjects were taking well to white civilization, a *Natal Witness* editorial contended that learning to plow and build would improve the "kaffir in the midst of Pondoland," who otherwise exploits women and spends every day "stupid with beer or gorged with flesh like a vulture or boa-constrictor." Such deeply racist depictions show how greed and rapaciousness were convenient placeholders for representing human and nonhuman bodies in colonial sites. They used animal characteristics to rationalize the civilizing mission and unevenly distributed the nature of uncivilized excess among different subject populations and their nonhuman cohabitants.

Missionaries, Orientalists, and hunters showed newer ways of knowing the vulture in the colonies. At the Asiatic Society in Ceylon in 1868, the colonial hunter-explorer Sir Samuel White Baker described how vultures find carrion by sight, not smell. Hiding a carcass underneath a bush and observing the behavior of vultures in Africa, he noticed that they would arrive at the scene of a carcass only if they witnessed its death. In African oral traditions, the vulture has also held a prominent place as a source of proverbial knowledge, which missionaries used to understand customary ideas. In March 1905, a missionary recounted a Gedeboe proverb in Monrovia's *Liberia Recorder*: "the vulture says—'consider your condition before you swallow a palm nut,' *mean-*

ing never vaunt unless your condition be bettered." In colonial India, the vulture's association with entrails lent itself to missionary discourses against intoxication. They often argued that alcohol consumed the Indian subject from the inside like a vulture would. Orientalists, on the other hand, dwelt on the figure of *Jatayu* in the Sanskrit epic poem *Ramayana*, describing him as a vulture god or vulture king in their translations or annotations of the text—a characterization that continues to this day.

In the European epic tradition, having stolen fire and given it to man, Zeus condemned Prometheus to an endless cycle of a vulture devouring his liver every day, beginning anew each morning. This myth was deployed to signify the sacrifices made by imperial rulers and colonists and the repeated assaults on symbols of imperial rule by anti-colonial actors. In Europe, the myth also fueled nationalist discourses. The Christian republican and ceaseless campaigner for Italian unification, Giuseppe Mazzini, famously opened his 1852 pamphlet *Duties of the Democracy* with the words "We have told truth enough to our enemies: thanks to us and to their own consciences, it now rends their hearts like the Vulture of Prometheus." The pamphlet and Mazzini's other writings would go on to spur nineteenth-century liberalism and anti-colonial nationalism in India.

Warships in the British Empire were commonly named after vultures, symbolizing the bird's predatory strength and relentlessness. In March 1847, Sir John Francis Davis bombed Canton from aboard the *Vulture* to wrest land on either side of the river for two additional factories and a church. In July 1854, a different HMS *Vulture* was pulverized by Russian batteries in the Baltic Sea harbor off the modern Finnish city of Kokkola. The *Spectator* ruefully recounted the loss of fifty-four men, a paddle box boat, and its twenty-four-pounder howitzer. Although it was a smaller theatre in the Crimean War, the wide reportage on the loss was used to rouse Britons into supporting the war. In May 1873, as governor of Bombay, Sir Henry Bartle Frere proudly commissioned yet another HMS *Vulture*. Stationed in the Persian Gulf, this vessel was to join a fleet from Bombay, sailing to put an end to the slave trade in Zanzibar and east Africa. Frere was subsequently appointed High Commissioner of South Africa, thanks in part to his role in the bombing of Zanzibar and the subsequent negotiations with its Sultan.

The vulture's intelligence also informed narratives by Britons opposed to war. The Society for the Promotion of Permanent and Universal Peace, formed in 1816, argued that war was not in line with the principles of Christianity. It remained an active pacifist organization until the 1930s as the London Peace Society. Their first pamphlet, titled *A solemn review of the custom of war, showing that war is the effect of popular delusion, and proposing a remedy* began with a piece by one Dr. Johnson that had formerly appeared in *The Idler*. Entitled *Conversation of the Vultures*, it used the figure of a Bohemian shepherd who could understand birds to narrate a conversation between a vulture mother and her children about their relationship with man. Even though men could not be killed as prey, the vulture mother told her children, they often warred with each other, leaving bodies maimed and dismembered for the convenience of vultures. On being asked why man doesn't eat what he kills, she relayed another wise vulture's view: that men weren't animals but "just vegetables, with the power of motion," who clashed like the branches of a tree in a storm until they lost their motion. Other vultures, she said, had noticed that "one in each herd gives directions to the rest" and seemed to be delighted by carnage: "he is seldom the biggest or swiftest but he shows in his eagerness and diligence that he is more than any other, a friend to the vulture." Johnson's allegorical tale held lessons that would go unheard through the nineteenth century, as Britain continued to scramble for military supremacy across the empire. Indeed, the tale hasn't outlived its relevance today. War continues apace. The vulture's name signifies newer forms of predation such as vulture funds and vulture capital—the money used by international financial institutions to buy weak companies or the debts of poorer nation-states.

Suggestions for Further Reading

"Africa's Vulture Populations Plummet." *Science* 348, 6242 (2015): 1405–6.

Balleisen, Edward. "Vulture Capitalism in Antebellum America: The 1841 Federal Bankruptcy Act and the Exploitation of Financial Distress." *Business History Review* 70, 4 (1996): 473–516.

Ogada, Darcy, Felicia Keesing, and Munir Virani. "Dropping Dead: Causes and Consequences of Vulture Population Declines Worldwide." *Annals of the New York Academy of Sciences* 1249, 1 (2012): 57–71.

Royte, Elizabeth. "Bloody Good." *National Geographic*, January 2016, 70–79, 88–97.

Scott-Heron, Gil. *The Vulture*. 1970. New York: Grove, 2010.

Sharafi, Mitra. "Entrusting the Faith: Religious Trusts and the Parsi Legal Profession." In *Law and Identity in Colonial South Asia: Parsi Legal Culture, 1772–1947*, 239–71. Cambridge, UK: Cambridge University Press, 2014.

Sidhwa, Bapsi. *The Crow Eaters*. Minneapolis: Milkweed, 1992 [1978].

Van Dooren, Thom. *Vulture*. London: Reaktion, 2011.

Vernon, Sally. "Trouble Up at t'Mill: The Rise and Decline of the Factory Play in the 1830s and 1840s." *Victorian Studies* 20, 2 (1977): 117–39.

"The Vulture." *Merry's Museum and Parley's Magazine* 22 (January–June 1852): 32.

Whitman, Charles. "The Birds of Old English Literature." *Journal of Germanic Philology* 2, 2 (1898): 149–98.

V is also for . . .

Vervet monkey
Vicuña
Viper
Vole

is for

WHALE

E ncumbered with an excess of religious and political flesh, the outsized whale was as symbolic as it was instrumental in British and American imperial ambitions in the oceans of the world. Water-borne mammals or air-breathing fish, whales straddled conceptual categories and had long been swaddled in myth. The Greek sea monster, Cetus, was sent by Poseidon to devour Andromeda in order to avenge Cassiopeia's maternal boast that his nymphs were less beautiful than her daughter. In the Jewish Torah, the suffering Job asks whether he is beseeched by God's sea monster, Leviathan. Later, the whale became a common sign of Satan for Christians. Conversely, Cetus was also seen as Jesus, the redeemer of the Christian fishes, a force for moral leadership, and an irresistible sign of the divinity and necessity of absolutist authority. Thomas Hobbes' influential political theology drew from this other meaning: the divine watery threat of Leviathan is symbolic of the terrifying power of the sovereign to overcome the terrestrial monstrosity of the civil war of all against all. The whale held the cultural and political imaginations of many Indigenous peoples of the Pacific, as well. Whales were repositories of spiritual power for some Northern peoples who hunted them, and ancestors and spiritual guides within some accounts of Polynesian settlement. Once

....

From Henry T. Cheever, *The Whale and His Captors; or, The Whaleman's Adventures* (Boston: Lathrop, 1850).

long-term provisioning of ships became possible in the mid-eighteenth century and imperialist endeavors came to depend on whale-hunting, British and American forays into new whaling grounds in the Pacific would engage these conflicting political and spiritual meanings (see also N IS FOR NORTH ATLANTIC RIGHT WHALE).

The gargantuan fleshiness of whales was more than symbolic freight. Whales migrated throughout the Pacific, efficiently transferring to tropical waters within their copious fat the concentrated energy of puny krill and other small creatures grown abundant in the long polar summers. Cetaceans, and pinnipeds like seals who evolved in the Pacific, linked the distant human communities and cultures of the Northern peoples who depended on them for sustenance and who followed their movements. The traffic of whales thus created oceanic encounters long before whales became the traffic of imperial trade. Indeed, the imperial whale trade depended on appropriating Indigenous knowledge about how to hunt and where to find whales. In the nineteenth century, people from the north Pacific were kidnapped and cajoled by imperial powers to set up communities as far south as Mexico to hunt sea mammals for the benefit of international trade. Patterns of imperial movement depended as much on animal migration as they did on political design. For whales who unwittingly helped spread this imperial economy in the nineteenth century, the entire Pacific became a dangerous and threatening home.

For British, American, and other imperial powers, refined whale oil was instrumental in creating modern "civilization" that helped legitimate imperial ambition. Whale oil provided a clean source of light in Europe from the middle ages through the eighteenth century, eponymously marking the Enlightenment with a product predominantly seized from the oceans of the so-called new world. Whale oil lubricated the machines and engines of the Industrial Revolution that began in Britain thereafter. Whale bone, baleen, and ivory were integral in the manufacture of umbrellas, corsets, tools, and other objects of mass production. If these material signs of civilization increasingly depended on the bodies of whales in the nineteenth century, so, too, did the subjectivity of the civilized person. Women's straight-laced restraint was symbolically fortified by whalebone-reinforced dress. Men imaginatively confronted both cetacean and "savage" monstrosities in their efforts to keep the oil flowing. They risked death by a powerful and intelligent animal escaping its pursuers on the one hand, and (the projected) fear of "savage" cannibalism in the tropical Pacific on the other.

Extracting resources and distancing the self from natural perils and uncontrolled "primitive" desires were the hallmarks of this civilization.

If the body of the whale created the material and symbolic conditions for thinking about western political sovereignty in Hobbes's time, the whale-hunting of the nineteenth century helped produce ideas central to imperial sovereignty. The conflicts among European and American fleets disturbed the prevalent beliefs that the ocean was free of territorial claims. Indigenous peoples throughout the Pacific did not share these assumptions. They had means to protect oceanic territories, including clearing the ocean floor to farm oysters, clams, and fish, factual contradictions to John Locke's influential arguments for why Indigenous peoples did not and could not own their lands. The imperial chasing of whales—and, certainly, the whales who were chased—provoked oceanic political boundaries and helped to create a law of property conducive to colonial ambition. In *Moby-Dick*, written at the peak of whale-hunting, Herman Melville notes the law of "fast-fish, loose-fish." This legal norm meant that a physical link, such as a harpoon line, holding fast a hunted whale made that animal property of the boat on the other end. But he also understood the colonial implications of such a law of property. "What was America in 1492 but a Loose-Fish? . . . What at last will Mexico be to the United States?" he mused.

Melville's character, Ahab, who personifies the monstrous quest to subdue leviathan and create a world of avenging justice, was himself sovereign. As captain of his ship *Pequod* (named for a violently defeated Indian nation not far from the New England home of the whaling fleet) he was an absolute sea king. Having lost a leg to the jaws of the great whale Moby-Dick, he wore a prosthesis of whale bone. This assemblage of man and beast signified the vital importance of whale flesh for the possibilities of sovereignty in the nineteenth century. The novel slyly shows how the whale's body not only upholds Ahab as the sovereign head of the ship, but also engages the busy activity of the partly Native and globally diverse crew collectively rendering the flesh of the whale's head—an emergent democratic idea of sovereignty that has subdued beast, "savage," and king alike.

Whaling's decline in the mid-nineteenth century was a direct result of massive industrial harvesting of whales and, eventually, the displacement of whale oil by petroleum. But its indelible history made American "manifest destiny" inclusive of oceans and the peoples and nations within them. American global imperialism was fused with national identity as well as international commerce and conquest, with devastating consequences for Indigenous communities and animal habitats.

By the late nineteenth century, the scarcity of whales, and overharvesting of fish and pinnipeds more generally, further weakened Indigenous communities that depended on ocean resources. In many cases, established treaties governing the hunting of whales and taking of fish were effectively nullified. As the American conservation movement took off in response to rapid declines of wild animals and forests, it called for emulation of Native peoples represented as ecologically noble, signifiers of natural harmony. In the twentieth century, some conservation struggles brought together Native activists reasserting treaty rights with concerned settlers distressed by the industrial slaughter of animals and misuse of land. Native peoples sometimes relied on the romanticized image of the ecological Indian themselves when it was politically efficacious, until it became apparent that this strategy reinforced state management over their lands and seas.

By early 1970, the image of the endangered whale spouted life into the environmentalist movement. The reckless overfishing of whales became a sign of all that was wrong with an intolerable and uncivilized relationship with the environment, culminating in the international moratorium on whaling in 1986. The cry to "Save the Whales" in order to save ourselves from destruction and from barbarism (whales were used for military target practice against imagined submarines) rearranged the hideous image of the whale from ancient times. No longer monstrous misfits, whales were frequently understood within environmentalist discourse to straddle the human/animal boundary, sharing language, intelligence, and empathy with humans. Whales reconstituted religious teachings and political power, legitimating governmental and scientific regulation of the natural environment. The growing industry of whale-watching and the sentimentalized anthropomorphism propounded by Sea World and aquariums allowed people to revel in what was once reviled.

Native challenges to their romanticized and subordinate place within settler colonial theories of scientific land and ocean management reached a zenith in 1999, with the decision of the Makah people of the Olympic peninsula to exercise their treaty rights to hunt and kill a whale. Popular anger with this decision revealed an incommensurate sovereign relationship that some Natives had to whales, which had been suppressed by aspirational images of harmony with nature provided by efforts to save the whales. Witi Ihimaera's novel *The Whale Rider*, Linda Hogan's *People of the Whale*, and Amitav Ghosh's *The Hungry Tide* sought to capture this new relationship to whales and other cetaceans, resisting romanticism as they explored the local, Indigenous meanings that make whales so important to anticolonial histories and practices.

Suggestions for Further Reading

Callahan, Richard J., Jr. "Whales, Cannibals, and Second Nature." *J19: The Journal of Nineteenth-Century Americanists* 3, 1 (2015): 190–97.

Ghosh, Amitav. *The Hungry Tide*. Boston: Houghton Mifflin Harcourt, 2005.

Hogan, Linda. *People of the Whale*. New York: Norton, 2008.

Honig, Bonnie. "Charged: Debt, Power, and the Politics of the Flesh in Shakespeare's *Merchant*, Melville's *Moby-Dick*, and Eric Santner's *The Weight of All Flesh*." In *The Weight of All Flesh: On the Subject-Matter of Political Economy*, edited by Kevis Goodman,131–82. Berkeley Tanner Lectures. Oxford: Oxford University Press, 2015.

Ihimaera, Witi. *The Whale Rider*. Auckland: Reed, 1987.

Jones, Ryan Tucker. "Running into Whales: The History of the North Pacific from Below the Waves." *American Historical Review* 118, 2 (2013): 349–77.

Melville, Herman. *Moby-Dick; or, The Whale*. New York: Harper, 1851.

Nadasdy, Paul. "Transcending the Debate over the Ecologically Noble Indian: Indigenous Peoples and Environmentalism." *Ethnohistory* 52, 2 (2005): 291–331.

Reid, Joshua L. *The Sea Is My Country: The Maritime World of the Makahs*. New Haven, CT: Yale University Press, 2015.

Rouleau, Brian. *With Sails Whitening Every Sea: Mariners and the Making of an American Maritime Empire*. Ithaca, NY: Cornell University Press, 2014.

Schmitt, Carl. *The Leviathan in the State Theory of Thomas Hobbes: Meaning and Failure of a Symbol*. Westport, CT: Greenwood, 1996.

W is also for . . .

Weasel
Wolf
Worm

is for

XERUS

*X*erus is the genus for various species of squirrel of the *Scur-idae* family and *Xerinae* subfamily found across the African continent. These include the Cape ground squirrel *Xerus inauris* found in South Africa and Namibia; the unstriped squirrel *Xerus rutilus* common to Kenya, Uganda, and Tanzania; and the Damara ground squirrel *Xerus princeps*, found usually in Angola. The sandy-colored white-striped ground squirrel, *Xerus erythropus*, often called *kidiri* in Swahili, is described in Jonathan Kingdon's *East African Mammals* as "bold and inquisitive." Further, he noted, even though "they walk in an unhurried manner, with frequent pauses for sniffing or peering about, they can run very fast in a continuous series of long leaps." While each *Xerus* species has morphological similarities with another, they also have strong differences. For instance, the *Xerus*

....

"Charming the Squirrel." From Paul Belloni Du Chaillu, *Wildlife under the Equator, Narrated for Young People* (New York: Harper, 1869). Photo © British Library Board, HMNTS 10095.bb.42.

princeps is found in rocky and dry mountains and is much more reclusive than the *Xerus inauris*. The sociality of the *Xerus inauris*, which is sex-segregated, has been described by the biologist Jane Waterman as "highly amicable;" among the female groups, she found no "evident dominance hierarchy." The *Xerus erythropus* is differentiated among several subspecies, especially by fur and hair. Darker pelages are common to *erythropus* subspecies in parts of Africa with more tropical climate; those inhabiting drier regions have lighter fur.

In African oral traditions, the squirrel's innocence and diligence made it a familiar carrier of moral ideas. In a popular Ghanaian trickster tale, a squirrel secretly farms a cornfield during a famine. His friend Anansi discovers it and he paves a road from his home to the farm to steal the corn. Squirrel sues him in court but is unable to prove how he reached his farm by climbing trees. Through Anansi's claim that the road proved his ability and intention to "tend to the farm," the parable dwells upon themes of trust and greed. It also points to a colonial modernity that privileged private property and the court as a site for negotiating the relationship between land, self, and community, often with unjust outcomes. In an older telling, a spider lines the road to squirrel's secret farm with webs and earthenware to prove that his family had used it. Although the judge returns the same verdict, the tale ends with a crow stealing the corn from the spider. The court fails in giving the squirrel justice, but a larger moral lesson is delivered: thieving does no one any good.

Missionaries used such oral traditions as passages toward advancing their understanding of African knowledge. Missionary orthographers in 1905 recounted a proverb—"the squirrel says, 'a two-year-old boy is an old man,' meaning the child should know that there were others who never reached that age before they died." The saying was popular among the Gedeboe in Liberia who, it was claimed, even derived their name from their Indigenous word for squirrel, *gede*. In the *Mombasa Diocesan*, a missionary related English proverbs to a popular Giryama proverb: "the squirrel is not chased out of two thickets," he wrote, "is a very good equivalent of our 'once bit twice shy.'" Translating African knowledge into terms relatable to Europeans was helpful in governing colonized peoples, and the squirrel was an unwitting intermediary.

The squirrel was an adorable cohabitant to white settlers in Africa until increasing populations led to assaults on settler farms in the early twentieth century. While newspapers reported on squirrels overbreeding due to warm winters, their readership was often ambivalent, if not disagreeable. Some cited—in contrast to England, where squirrels were posing similar problems—the existence of more natural predators like owls and hawks in the Cape that could keep squirrel populations low. Others deflected blame from the squirrel toward more objectionable colonial designs. On September 25, 1913, the *Bulawayo Chronicle* syndicated a column by the suggestively named "Sciurus," accusing Cecil Rhodes of introducing the squirrel from England and enabling its pestilence. "There were squirrels in Northern Africa before we got them and these may be now quietly spreading south to join up with their brothers," Sciurus claimed, "just as the railway is going to link up with Rhodes' other scheme." Rhodes, the author contended, may have won over skeptics with his Cape to Cairo railroad design; but the squirrels would accompany that fantasy as a nightmare worse than the Pharaonic plague, hindering the empire's pan-African ambitions. All hope was not lost, Sciurus wrote. Squirrels of European heritage still possessed ancestral traits of "activity and industry" which had "done no great harm to the farmer in Europe," but instead supplied "many pretty women with fine fur coats."

Squirrel fur was an important commodity in colonial Africa. Since the 1830s, the expansion of the fur industry had turned squirrel-hunting from a European pastime into a means of resource extraction. In 1839, South Africa's *Grahamstown Journal* would carry regular front-page advertisements for "fashionable furs" sold by R. H. Caffyn, a trader in Liberian squirrel furs. Liberia, then a newly engineered West African colony, had quickly become a popular source of coarse but bushy squirrel furs for markets in other parts of Africa. Besides its use for fur, white settlers in Liberia also emphasized the squirrels' place in the diet of Africans. In his book *Liberia*, the geographer Sir Harry Johnston casually observed that "natives and Americo-Liberians" regularly "appreciated the flesh of these [large Central African] squirrels, partly because of their rich fattening diet." By 1856, other traders, such as Charles Mallett, began selling squirrel furs dyed in various colors to suit the needs of both fashion and climate in the Cape Colony. Consumers of such squirrel furs were mostly women. With the expanding circulation of newspapers and periodicals, garments considered fashionable in Europe's cities found keen consumers among women in the colonies. (On women's fashion, see also K IS FOR KIWI; W IS FOR WHALE.) Due to its coarseness, squirrel fur was a cheaper alternative to other furs, especially for women with limited incomes. Madame Aimee May argued as much in the *Rhodesian Herald* on December 25, 1908: for women "who traverse the sombre streets on foot," the squirrel fur was a "skin of utility."

Squirrels were also hunted across British settler colonies because many considered them good for hunting practice—while its agility was a challenge, at least it was not too slippery, unlike Australian flying foxes. In 1909, Charles "Buffalo" Jones, the Illinois-born bison hunter and first game warden of Yellowstone Park, decided to go to east Africa to "rope lions" for zoos in the United States. In an interview from London that appeared in Mombasa's *East African Standard* on February 26, 1910, he said, "when I was twelve years old, I caught my first squirrel. It bit my finger but I sold it for two dollars. Since then, I've been chasing everything on four legs trying to get a fortune. And I'm still at it." Masculinity for young white men in frontier territories was often shaped by successes at squirrel-hunting, then considered a gateway to the more mature aptitude necessary for big game (see T IS FOR TIGER).

The death of African squirrels symbolized colonialism in craftier ways. Take, for instance, an illustration in the 1869 children's book *Wildlife under the Equator, Narrated for Young People*, by French American colonial anthropologist Paul Du Chaillu. Among the Bakalai in the French Congo forests, the self-styled "chevalier errant" who went to "unknown countries where no white man had gone before," recounted falling acutely sick. In the larger narrative centered on the white savior with "deep love for these wild men," the illness suddenly reveals his vulnerability and his dependence on Africans around him for everything. Du Chaillu is left craving his former strength, implicitly to regain his position as benefactor. Still very feeble, with no Bakalai men around, Du Chaillu suffers a moment of helplessness when he spots a squirrel being "charmed by a snake." After weeks spent battling snakes elsewhere, once even to feed the hungry African slaves accompanying him, Du Chaillu yearned to similarly protect the "nice and beautiful" squirrel from the "shiny and ugly" snake. His failure to do so rendered the "poor little squirrel" a lasting animal metonym for the primitive African figure in need of the protection of a white presence, whose sense of self could only be (re)acquired by successfully "saving" the colonized.

Among other British colonists, the squirrel received both admiration and mockery. Horse breeders in the Cape Colony admired its speed and placidity, naming many winning racehorses after squirrels. Elsewhere, its steadiness on trees appeared in settler narratives across the British Empire. In March 1907, Johannesburg's *Rand Daily Mail* carried the travelogue of a settler gold-miner in Canada. Calling himself a Londoner, he recounted how his trek to the "unexplored" Larder Lake in northern Ontario was interrupted by howling wolves which he fantastically escaped by climbing up a tree: "A squirrel might have envied my agility at the moment." In Maine, the Squirrel was a popular whisky. In 1908, at the opening of Dewar House on London's Haymarket Street, Sir Thomas Dewar, owner of the global liquor distillers Messrs. Dewar and Sons, mockingly derided it as cheap competition. It was, he declared, made of wood alcohol, mellowed by glycerin, and infused with tobacco. When asked why it was called the Squirrel then, he remarked, "I guess it's because the men who drink it talk 'nutty' and climb trees." Incidentally, in the United States, *Xerus* in particular had another life as an embodiment of excellence and responsibility for young children. Carolyn Wells's famous *Alphabet Antics*, carried by the Boston-based *Youth's Companion* on August 1, 1901, held the following entry for the letter X: "X was a Xerus, with a long tail; He carried his Luncheon to school in a pail. Excellent Xerus!"

In England, however, young Britons were more familiar with the red and gray squirrels. In children's literature, the squirrel's restlessness had long conveyed a love of liberty. The earliest example of this was the popular 1807 book *The Adventures of a Squirrel, Supposed to Be Related by Himself*, which taught a young Anne kindness toward a squirrel that had escaped cages, violent schoolboys, and "gipsies" from Southampton to the streets of London. The squirrel was also an expert navigator, according to the *Boy's Play-Book of Science* by Professor Pepper. Among skilled animals like bees and caterpillars, it said, the squirrel was a "ferryman, with a piece of bark for a boat and his tail for a sail." It exhorted English boys to learn from such animals but not forget that only man has the "god-like attributes of mind and thought" required to compete with other "nations of men." With the publication of Beatrix Potter's *Tale of Squirrel Nutkin* in 1903, the red squirrel (incorrectly considered indigenous to England) became a fond repository of idyllic Englishness. Nutkin sailed on twig boats in the Lake District, battled a mighty owl, and learned a moral lesson by losing his most prized possession, his tail.

In 2017, under royal patronage, the United Kingdom formalized many measures to increase the endangered red squirrel population, including culling the "invasive" American gray squirrel, thus buttressing the red's Englishness. The African squirrel, on the other hand, still doesn't need saving. In 2017, the *Xerus inauris* showed University of Zurich biologists complex abilities, using the sun's position and angles of shadows to navigate between hidden stores of food in the Kalahari's most arid stretches.

Suggestions for Further Reading

Coates, Peter. "Creatures Enshrined: Wild Animals as Bearers of Heritage." *Past and Present* 226, S. 10 (2015): 272–98.

Flower, William Henry, and Richard Lydekker. *An Introduction to the Study of Mammals Living and Extinct*. London: Black, 1891.

Insaidoo, Kwame. *Moral Lessons in African Folktales*. Vol.1. Bloomington, IN: Authorhouse, 2011.

Jenkins, Elwyn. *National Character in South African English Children's Literature*. London: Routledge, 2006.

Kean, Hilda. "Imagining Rabbits and Squirrels in the English Countryside." *Society and Animals* 9 (2001): 164.

Kingdon, Jonathan, David Happold, Michael Hoffman, Thomas Butynski, Meredith Happold, and Jan Kalina. *Mammals of Africa*. Vols. 1–6. London: Bloomsbury, 2013.

Monadjem, Ara, Peter Taylor, Christiane Denys, and Fenton Cotterill. *Rodents of Sub-Saharan Africa: A Biogeographic and Taxonomic Synthesis*. Berlin: De Gruyter, 2015.

Nemy, Enid. "ABCs on the Wall: African Bestiary." *New York Times*, June 15, 1977, 57.

Waterman, Jane. "The Social Organization of the Cape Ground Squirrel *Xerus Inauris*." *Ethology* 101 (1995): 130–47.

Woodson, Carter. *African Myths*. New York: Associated, 1948.

X is also for . . .

Xenarthra
Xenopus
X-ray tetra

is for

YAK

The yak's tail was its prize, but watch out for its horns. Across southern Asia, flywhisks made from yak tails had been valued possessions since antiquity. Scholars in the eighteenth and nineteenth centuries found references to yak tails and royalty in older Sanskrit and Buddhist texts; others studied Aelian's *De Natura Animalium*, a third-century Roman compendium. Aelian described a timid, herbivorous animal in India, with a bushy tail of hair that grew like a tassel. When hunted, the animal "hides its tail in some thicket, faces about, and stands waiting for its pursuers and plucks up its courage, fancying that, since its tail is not visible, it will no longer seem worth pursuing. For it knows that its beauty resides in its tail."

As governor-general of Bengal in the 1770s, Warren Hastings employed a large retinue of servants to brush flies from the air with yaktails. Hastings hoped to breed yaks in Calcutta, and his wish list for George Bogle's diplomatic mission to the Himalayas in 1774 included animals that produced wool for shawls or tails for whisks. The yaks died

....

"The Yak of Tartary," by George Stubbs. From Samuel Turner, *An Account of an Embassy to the Court of the Teshoo Lama, in Tibet* (London: Bulmer, 1800). Courtesy of Houghton Library, Harvard University.

on route, although several cashmere-wool-producing goats returned to Hastings's paddock. A report in *Philosophical Transactions* lauded the beautiful, long-flowing hairs of the "cow-tails." The value of these increased when "mounted on silver handles, for Chrowras, or brushes, to chase away the flies; and no man of consequence in India ever goes out, or sits in form at home, without two Chowrawbadars, or brushers, attending him, with such instruments in their hands." Thomas Pennant's 1781 *History of Quadrupeds* added that the tails were used to ornament the ears of elephants, dyed red to adorn Chinese bonnets, and mentioned frequently in sacred books of the Mongols.

Pennant relied on Bogle's authority to confirm older fables of cow-tails and the more recent Linnaean classification of the "grunting ox." Yaks had long been crossbred with domestic cows in the high plateaus of central Asia, and their milk and cheese were as valued locally as their meat, skins, hair, and tails. Pennant warned that "even when subjugated, they retain their fierce nature." The sight of bright colors might lead them to attack; a wounded yak would pursue assailants and toss them in the air by their horns. Owners cut off the sharp points of the horns "to prevent mischief."

Hastings received a pair of yaks from Bhutan in 1784 from Samuel Turner, his cousin and an East India Company army officer, whom he had sent on a trade mission. Turner's account of this journey introduced the yak of Tartary, or the bushy-tailed bull of Tibet, to a wider audience. When Hastings returned to England in 1785, his collection of animals stayed behind in Alipore, where they formed the core of the governor's menagerie and later Calcutta Zoo's.

Once in England, Hastings faced severe criticism and a lengthy impeachment trial for his methods of rule in Bengal, and he sought consolation by shipping his yaks from Calcutta. Hastings purchased his family's ancestral estate at Daylesford, which he tore down to build a mansion in the "Mughal style." It was filled with Indian objects and surrounded by a large park, with yaks, shawl goats, and exotic plants. His female yak died during the sea voyage, but the bull survived and became something of a celebrity. Hastings commissioned George Stubbs to paint the yak's portrait, along with paintings of Hastings on his Arabian horse.

The image of Hastings's yak from Turner's *Account of an Embassy to the Court of the Teshoo Lama in Tibet* reproduces Stubbs's painting of the yak in profile, with white tail and tousled hair, in its native habitat in Bhutan. In the background, mountains rise above Punakha

Dzong—"the palace of great happiness"—reflected in a lake. In the foreground, the vegetables under the yak's nose are the Bhutan turnip, which Hastings admired and planted in his English garden.

The tale of Hastings's yak became one of dissent after its arrival in England. Samuel Turner reported that the yak was initially "in a torpid languid state" but adjusted to the climate and "recovered at once both his health and vigor." This bull eventually fathered many calves, but in early days was said to resent its ill treatment during the voyage and harbor a hostility toward horses—and, perhaps, its owners. A knob nailed into the yak's horn rubbed off, but the crooked nail remained stuck in its horn and "happened to gore a valuable coach-horse belonging to Mr. Hastings, which had the range of the same pasture with him, and, lacerating the entrails, occasioned his death. After this, to prevent further accidents, he was kept alone within a secure enclosure."

Hastings's yak may have been fenced in, but Stubbs's image circulated for decades. The anatomist John Hunter commissioned a copy of the yak portrait from Stubbs, which was displayed prominently in his Leicester Square "museum" and later in the Royal College of Surgeons. Access to the Himalayas was limited, so this portrait remained the European model for a yak for the next half-century. In the 1840s, Abbé Huc, a French missionary priest, memorably described Tibetan snow-covered yaks in winter looking "as if they were preserved in sugar candy." According to the German physician Werner Hoffmeister, to ride a yak was to be in fear of a "kick with their hind-feet, turning their heads round perpetually, as if about to gore their riders."

By the mid-nineteenth century, European observers saw yaks more often in menageries or taxidermy exhibits than in the wild (see L IS FOR LION). The zoologist Edward Blyth used his position as curator for the Asiatic Society of Bengal to trade in exotic animals with Indian princes and British collectors. Around 1848, Blyth sold a yak to the Earl of Derby to join a hybrid yak in the menagerie at Knowsley Hall, near Liverpool. When the menagerie was auctioned in 1851, the hybrid yak thrived at Belle Vue Gardens in Manchester, but the purebred yak was bought by a showman and died shortly afterward, cooped up in a caravan. The most famous yaks of midcentury were the dozen shipped by a French diplomat from Shanghai to Paris in 1854. Most of these yaks were exhibited in the acclimatization gardens of the Bois de Boulogne, while a few were sent to the Alps in hopes of adapting them to alpine agriculture.

Stuffed yaks were frequently on display. By the 1850s, taxidermy specimens were exhibited at Edinburgh, Liverpool, and Calcutta and at the British Museum, East India Museum, and Crystal Palace in London. At the Crystal Palace, yaks were the centerpiece of an ethnographic diorama about Tibetans. In these imperial displays, the exoticism of the yak and the empire were brought together under British and European control. In 1855, *Crystal Palace Alphabet: A Guide for Good Children*, included this entry: "Y stands for Yak, whose tails from Thibet / On Turkish high officers' caps are now set."

The domestication of the yak in the British imagination was seemingly complete by 1896, with Hilaire Belloc's *The Bad Child's Book of Beasts*. Its whimsical illustrations and doggerel verses described the yak as a child's friend and pet for centuries in Tibet. In rhyme, children could ride the yak or lead it with a string: "Then tell your papa where the Yak can be got, / And if he is awfully rich / He will buy you the creature— or else he will *not*."

In the Himalayas, however, such juvenilia paled beside the pathetic fate of yaks during the British invasion of Tibet, led by Francis Younghusband in 1903–1904. According to Perceval Landon, these yaks were "one of the dreariest histories of a waste of animal life in military records." The expedition started with 3,500 yaks carrying loads, adding at least 1,000 more yaks while in Tibet; yet fewer than 200 survived by the end of the journey. The expedition did not provide fodder, so the yaks had to forage on their own in the arid climate. The lesson for Landon was "never again to place their reliance upon these burly and delicate beasts."

British mountaineers learned to provide forage and relied on yaks to cross Tibet to Mount Everest in the 1920s and 1930s. Human porters replaced yaks when the climbing shifted from Tibet to Nepal in the 1950s. Western climbers then viewed yaks as a picturesque backdrop or the source of dung for fires or meat for meals. Sherpa Tenzing Norgay, who had been a yak herder in the area as a boy, reached the summit of Everest with Edmund Hillary in 1953.

Yaks still serve as beasts of burden in the Himalayas, carrying goods across the mountains or hauling baggage for thousands of trekkers and climbers to Mount Everest Base Camp. The image of yaks for such visitors oscillates between domestication and disruption. The most popular path up Everest is derisively—and inaccurately—called the "yak route." But if yak tails have lost their luster, their sharp horns tell another tale. When encountering a yak on the trail, it is the humans who must hustle to get out of the way.

Suggestions for Further Reading

Aris, Michael. *Views of Medieval Bhutan: The Diary and Drawings of Samuel Davis 1783*. London: Serinda, 1982.

Harris, Tina. "Yak Tails, Santa Claus, and Transnational Trade in the Himalayas." *The Tibet Journal* 39, 1 (2014): 145–55.

Moore, Thomas John, and Edmund Smyth. "Notes on the Yak, or Grunting Ox, and Other Ruminating Animals from Central Asia." *Transactions of the Historic Society of Lancashire and Cheshire* 9 (1856–57): 43–60.

Nott, John Fortuné. *Wild Animals Photographed and Described*. London: Low, Marston, Searle, and Rivington, 1886.

Osborne, Michael A. *Nature, the Exotic, and the Science of French Colonialism*. Bloomington: Indiana University Press, 1994.

Qureshi, Sadiah. *Peoples on Parade: Exhibitions, Empire, and Anthropology in Nineteenth-Century Britain*. Chicago: University of Chicago Press, 2011.

Stewart, John. "An Account of the Kingdom of Thibet." *Philosophical Transactions of the Royal Society of London* 67 (1778): 465–92.

Turner, Samuel. *Account of an Embassy to the Court of the Teshoo Lama, in Tibet*. London, 1800.

Turner, Samuel. "Description of the Yak of Tartary, Called Soora-goy, or the Bushy-Tailed Bull of Tibet." *Asiatick Researches* 4 (1795): 351–53.

Y is also for . . .

Yabby
Yellow-backed duiker
Yeti
Yorkshire terrier

is for

ZEBU

The zebu (*Bos taurus indicus*) descends from an ancient South Asian species of cattle, possibly animals with both back and chest humps. Zebu cattle have been adapted for diverse purposes including milk, meat, and work. They are distinct from taurine cattle, which descend from the Fertile Crescent. More than thirty zebu breeds exist in India, where they feature in mythology and religious practices in both Hindu and Muslim populations. Non-Hindu peoples in India, Africa, and elsewhere value the zebu as food-producing property, as entertainment (bull-butting) and transportation, and for their manure, which is used as fertilizer and fuel. The neck hump, as seen in an 1882 woodcut, constitutes the animal's distinctive morphological feature, but it varies in size, shape, firmness, and location. Modern zebus are ordinarily back-humped with a hanging flap of neck skin (dewlap), and tend to have larger ears and appear more slender than taurine (*Bos taurus taurus*) cattle lines (see C IS FOR CATTLE, especially

....

"Zebu." From John George Wood, *The Illustrated Natural History* (Philadelphia: Crawford, 1883). Used by permission of Getty Images, object number: 182704160.

the woodcut illustration). The hump is a repository of fatty tissue and muscle. The voluminous skin of the hump and dewlap, and the animal's short hair, help it to regulate body temperature. Zebus are sometimes termed Brahman cattle—an ironic term as members of the present-day Brahmin caste in India and others following the Hindu religion are vegetarian and forbidden to butcher animals. The Brahman breed was developed in the United States from imported Indian animals. The zebu is a trans-imperial animal par excellence, and is now a widely dispersed breed. It has circulated far beyond its ancient and modern borders and beyond the modern Anglophone world. Zebus are also notable for their presence in domesticated form in premodern and modern empires. The animal is a survivor of imperialism. Its special musculature—the presence of a subcutaneous muscle—enables it to shake off insects and parasites more easily than taurine breeds. Thus, unlike most taurine breeds, zebus prosper in tropical and subtropical heat and disease environments. It is now prevalent on the Indian subcontinent and across central Africa, South America, the southern United States, and northern Australia.

Genetic analysis suggests that zebus were already distinct from taurine cattle about 330,000 years ago. They were domesticated in the Indus Valley of present-day Pakistan between 8,000 and 6,000 BCE. Their ancestors may have included the wild banteng (*Bos javanicus*) and possibly an Indian form of aurochs. Archaeological evidence suggests that zebus had an established role in culture about 4,000 years ago, when they appear as terracotta toys and in carvings. The Buddhist religion allowed milk-drinking, and dharma texts prior to the fifth century CE permitted consumption of cattle by Hindus. Hindu proscriptions against eating meat were in place by the eleventh century CE. Later, British imperial efforts to introduce cattle-eating and slaughterhouses into India had diverse impacts on the modern Hindu religion. Such efforts both bolstered British identity in the colonies and became sites of resistance to colonial rule.

The dispersion of zebus from South Asia to the Horn of Africa dates to the seventh century CE, but any "pure" form of the animal is likely lost in the depths of time and genomics. The zebu is interfertile with unhumped taurine cattle and with the African sanga. The latter animal is sometimes viewed as the result of crossing zebu and taurine breeds, although osteological research suggests sanga cattle are crossbreeds derived from indigenous wild bovids, such as the African buffalo. Some regions in Africa cultivate long-horned zebu varieties because the horns are used in funeral rituals, and varieties of zebus are widely dispersed on the continent. The Maasai peoples of East Africa include the zebu in rituals where a live animal's blood is consumed. The blood is promoted as an agent of health for children and the elderly. Although zebus are capable of carrying parasites contracted from tsetse fly bites, human blood-drinking practices have not been shown to transmit sleeping sickness or other disease-causing trypanosomes to humans.

Early modern and Enlightenment European naturalists and some agriculturalists were well aware of the zebu. The sixteenth-century physician and naturalist Prospero Alpini, who spent three years in Egypt as physician to the Venetian consul in Cairo, observed the animal's presence in Egypt and noted that they were said to have been brought from Asia. The Frenchman Pierre Belon published a print of a "Boeuf d'Afrique" in 1554, an animal with crescent-shaped horns, but without prominent humps or a pendulous dewlap. Two centuries later, the intendant of the King's Garden in Paris, Georges Buffon, noted that a "Boeuf de Belon" was shown at an agricultural fair in Paris; its handler identified it as a zebu, adding that it came from Africa. Buffon included an entry on the zebu in his *Histoire Naturelle* and noted the arrival of zebus at the royal menagerie at Versailles in August 1761. Like Belon, he published a print of the animal. He also took measurements of it and recorded them in his entry on the zebu, describing the animal as affectionate and good-natured. The term zebu stabilized around this time, but Buffon noted it was sometimes called the African Dant or Lant. He also recorded that zebus had been shipped to America. He warned readers not to confuse the zebu with either the camel, whose description immediately preceded it, or the tapir, which followed it. Buffon wrote in an era when both British and French East India companies were active in south Asia. Other companies, merchants, and adventurers targeted the island of Madagascar and other regions of Africa. The British, Dutch, and French competed with Spain and Portugal for early modern colonies. Because of these imperial networks and proximity to India, zebus became the most prominent cattle breed on the vast island of Madagascar. The French and British chartered crown companies formed the initial backbone of European commercial and cultural ties to south Asia and Africa. Their ships enabled the circulation of organisms, goods, and disease. A series of wars in the eighteenth century left Great Britain in control of most of France's older colonies, particularly those of southeast India.

In the wake of the English Civil War, English hatter and author of self-help manuals Thomas Tryon, and a few other political radicals, found fault with carnivorous diets and the consumption of alcohol and tobacco. Vegetarianism was seen as a way to treat the earth and all its inhabitants with greater care and compassion. Tryon, who encountered slavery in Barbados but did not set foot on the Asian subcontinent, celebrated Hindu vegetarianism and established a modest Brahmanic vegetarian community in London. He drew on Indian travelogues and Cornelius Agrippa's occult and magical practices to fashion a call for moral, dietary, and spiritual reform. The program combined pacifism with a curious amalgam of Orientalist philosophy, combining Pythagorean, Hindu, and Christian elements. In this way, he positioned vegetarianism as a key to spiritual enlightenment. Though not specifically addressing the zebu, Tryon advocated for what we would call animal rights. He did so as part of his belief in microcosm-macrocosm relationships and hidden sympathetic affinities between these two worlds.

Tryon's fringe ideas barely altered English dietary habits. In India, however, the practice of meat-eating had different cultural and political implications. Like famine and disease, the politics of meat consumption and the social unrest it caused became symbols of the impotence of the British Raj. In 1885, a retired British civil servant and several educated Indians convened the Indian National Congress to promote the participation of Indian people in their own governance. Hindus predominated in the Congress. In its wake, they staged a number of anti-cow-killing "riots" that sharpened boundaries between Hindus and Muslims on the one hand, and between Hindus and British on the other. The Muslim diet included beef, and tradition made cows a preferred animal for ceremonial sacrifice. Hindus reacted to these practices in various ways. In 1893, at Basantpur near Nepal, Hindus formed a Cow Protection Society. Other actions included founding an asylum for aged cows and burning down slaughterhouses. The politics of cows and meat-eating continues to affect an independent India. In 2016, India's richest state, Maharashtra, banned cow slaughter but allowed beef consumption if the animals were slaughtered out of state.

Beyond India, the zebu's modern history is linked to new agricultural, aesthetic, and cultural processes. Exported to North America before the U.S. Civil War, the zebu became simultaneously an agricultural animal fit for pastoralists and an exotic animal seen in zoos. In the 1870s, the Philadelphia Zoo exhibited as the sacred bull of India a black zebu sent from the Prospect Park Zoo in New York City. The animals were common to other zoo collections as well, and could be found in Amsterdam, Berlin, Chicago, Cincinnati, Hamburg, and many other cities. For example, the Paris Museum of Natural History exhibited a magnificent zebu bull named Massena in the 1930s. Earlier, another Paris zoo, the Jardin d'Acclimatation, had packaged and distributed milk from its zebu herd. Zebu breeds were coded frequently as exotic beasts and often given names and recognized as individuals. They were sometimes presented in zoos as symbols of imperial power or as examples of a resource successfully exploited and adapted by Europeans for the good of the colonizer and even of humanity in general. Zebus accompanied British, French, and Portuguese colonization efforts beyond India. Europeans believed that the African diet lacked meat, and that this rendered Africans less able to work in colonial enterprises. Dutch, German, and British settlers in eastern and southern Africa made significant investments in cattle culture. Early settlers regarded the zebu as inferior to the predominately taurine cattle breeds common in Europe. Initial attempts to improve herds—generally meaning meat production—with imported British and other European cattle ended in disaster. In 1902, after the Second Boer War, an outbreak of rinderpest decimated the sanga and "Afrikander" breed herds common in German East Africa and South Africa. British authorities contracted with the great German bacteriologist, Robert Koch, to study the outbreak and suppress it. South Africa reconstituted its herds with Brahman zebu stock developed in the United States. Brazil developed an Indo-Brazilian breed, which today accounts for 90 percent of the country's production., Other lines were developed and adapted for Panama, Columbia, Argentina, Paraguay, and the tropical climate of Northern Australia, where today about 50 percent of all Australian cattle derive from zebu.

The history of the zebu and its alteration and dispersal is entwined with premodern and modern colonialism, globalization, and commodification. Zebus are found in far corners of the British Commonwealth and in both hemispheres. Although occasionally seen in zoos today, zebus are more often viewed in fields, and at meetings and shows of cattle breeding clubs. The animal also appears in children's literature and is described by the poet and children's author Jane Yolen as "A cow—but not a cow—and how." In the United States, where the

American Brahman breed has been promoted since the 1930s, the U.S. Foreign Agricultural Service provides funds to assist with its international export. The zebu has also had a cameo role as a media star on the cartoon television series *The Simpsons*, in which Lisa Simpson used an image of one to expand the horizons of her younger sister, Maggie.

Suggestions for Further Reading

Akerman, Joe A. *American Brahman*. Houston: American Brahman Breeders Association, 1982.

Grigson, Caroline. "An African Origin for African Cattle? Some Archaeological Evidence." *African Archaeological Review* 9 (1991): 119–44.

Guerrini, Anita. "A Diet for a Sensitive Soul: Vegetarianism in Eighteenth-Century Britain." *Eighteenth-Century Life* 23, 2 (1999): 34–42.

Guerrini, Anita. "Health, National Character and the English Diet in 1700." *Studies in History and Philosophy of Biological and Biomedical Sciences* 43 (2012): 349–56.

Korom, Frank J. "Holy Cow! The Apotheosis of Zebu, or Why the Cow Is Sacred in Hinduism." *Asian Folklore Studies* 59, 2 (2000): 181–203.

Phillips, Ralph W. "Cattle." *Scientific American* 198, 6 (1958): 51–59.

Porto-Neto, Laercio R., Tad S. Sonstegard, George E. Liu, Derek M. Bickhart, Marcos V. B. Da Silva, Marco A. Achado, Yuri T. Utsunomiya, Jose F. Garcia, Cedric Gondo, and Curtis P. Van Tassel. "Genomic Divergence of Zebu and Taurine Cattle Identified through High-Density SNP Genotyping." *BMC Genomics* 14 (2013): 876.

Sanders, James O. "History and Development of Zebu Cattle in the United States." *Journal of Animal Science* 50, 6 (1980): 1188–1200.

Stuart, Tristram. *The Bloodless Revolution: A Cultural History of Vegetarianism from 1600 to Modern Times*. New York: Norton, 2006).

Yang, Anand A. "Sacred Symbol and Sacred Space in Rural India: Community Mobilization in the 'Anti-Cow Killing' Riot of 1893." *Comparative Studies in Society and History*, 22, 4 (1980): 576–96.

Z is also for...

Zebra
Zebra duiker
Zebra shark
Zebrafish
Zokor
Zorilla

CONTRIBUTORS

NEEL AHUJA (M IS FOR MOSQUITO) is Associate Professor of Feminist Studies and a core faculty member in the Critical Race and Ethnic Studies Program at the University of California, Santa Cruz. He is the author of *Bioinsecurities: Disease Interventions, Empire, and the Government of Species* (2016).

ANTOINETTE BURTON (COEDITOR; AUTHOR OF L IS FOR LION AND S IS FOR SCORPION) is Professor of History and Swanlund Chair at the University of Illinois at Urbana-Champaign. She is the editor of *An ABC of Queen Victoria's Empire* (2017) and coeditor, with Tony Ballantyne, of *World Histories from Below* (2016).

TONY BALLANTYNE (K IS FOR KIWI) is Professor of History and Pro-Vice-Chancellor, Humanities, at the University of Otago, where he is also codirector of the Centre for Research on Colonial Culture. He has published widely on empires in modern world history, the cultural history of the British Empire in the nineteenth century, and colonialism and its consequences in New Zealand. His most recent monograph is *Entanglements of Empire: Missionaries, Maori and the Question of the Body* (2014).

UTATHYA CHATTOPADHYAYA (U IS FOR UNICORN, V IS FOR VULTURE, AND X IS FOR *XERUS*) is Assistant Professor of History at the University of California, Santa Barbara, where he teaches courses on the history of South Asia, the British Empire, and the Indian Ocean world. He holds a Ph.D. in History from the University of Illinois at Urbana-Champaign.

ANNALIESE CLAYDON (B IS FOR BOAR AND P IS FOR PLATYPUS) received her Ph.D. in History from the University of Illinois at Urbana-Champaign in 2015. Her work examines the interactions between polar explorers' families, Indigenous intermediaries, and vernacular agents in the early mid-nineteenth century. Originally from Alaska, she now resides in Tasmania, where she is an archivist at the Tasmanian Archive and Heritage Office and a University Associate in the Department of History and Classics at the University of Tasmania.

....

.JONATHAN GOLDBERG-HILLER (W IS FOR WHALE) is Professor of Political Science at the University of Hawai'i at Mānoa, where he teaches sociolegal theory. He is the author of *The Limits to Union: Same-Sex Marriage and the Politics of Civil Rights* (2004) and *Plastic Materialities: Politics, Legality, and Metamorphosis in the Work of Catherine Malabou* (coedited with Brenna Bhandar, 2015). Goldberg-Hiller has published widely on issues of legal aesthetics, sexuality, and Indigenous rights. He is coeditor of a Duke University Press book series, Global and Insurgent Legalities, and former coeditor of the *Law and Society Review*. He is currently writing a book on the legal and political significance of night.

....

PETER H. HANSEN (Y IS FOR YAK) is Professor of History and Director of International and Global Studies at Worcester Polytechnic Institute.

He is the author of *The Summits of Modern Man: Mountaineering after the Enlightenment* (2013). He has written widely about mountaineering and modernity and has appeared on BBC television. Hansen is currently writing a history of commercialization and Mount Everest.

....

DANIEL HEATH JUSTICE (R IS FOR RACCOON) is a citizen of the Cherokee Nation. He is Professor of English and Canada Research Chair in Indigenous Literature and Expressive Culture in First Nations and Indigenous Studies at the University of British Columbia.

....

ISABEL HOFMEYR (J IS FOR JACKAL [AND DINGO]) is Professor of African Literature at the University of the Witwatersrand and Global Distinguished Professor at New York University. She has worked extensively on the Indian Ocean world and oceanic themes more generally. Recent publications include *Gandhi's Printing Press: Experiments in Slow Reading* (2013) and a special issue of *Comparative Literature* (2016) on "Oceanic Routes," coedited with Kerry Bystrom. She heads up a project, Oceanic Humanities for the Global South, with partners from Mozambique, Mauritius, India, Jamaica, and Barbados.

....

DANE KENNEDY (T IS FOR TIGER) is the Elmer Louis Kayser Professor of History and International Affairs at George Washington University, where he teaches world, British, and British imperial history. He is the author of numerous books, including *The Magic Mountains: Hill Stations and the British Raj* (1996), *The Highly Civilized Man: Richard Burton and the Victorian World* (2005), *The Last Blank Spaces: Exploring Africa and Australia* (2013), and *Decolonization: A Very Short Introduction* (2018).

....

JAGJEET LALLY (H IS FOR HORSE) is Lecturer in the History of Early Modern and Modern India at University College London (UCL) and codirector of the UCL Centre for the Study of South Asia and the Indian Ocean World. His interests range across the environmental, economic, social, and cultural history of the Indian subcontinent and Afro-Eurasia since 1500. He studied at Oxford, the London School of Economics, and Cambridge, where he received his Ph.D. He was subsequently a Moses and Mary Finley Research Fellow in History at Darwin College, and he has also taught at Imperial College, London.

....

KRISTA MAGLEN (N IS FOR NORTH ATLANTIC RIGHT WHALE) is Associate Professor in the History Department at Indiana University, Bloomington. Her current book project seeks to examine historic encounters and interactions with dangerous animals in Australian history. Her first book, *The English System: Quarantine, Immigration, and the Making of a Port Sanitary Zone* (2014) was shortlisted for the Royal Historical Society's Whitfield Prize.

....

AMY E. MARTIN (A IS FOR APE) is Professor of English on the Emma B. Kennedy Foundation at Mount Holyoke College. She is the author of *Alter-Nations: Nationalisms, Terror, and the State in Nineteenth Century Britain and Ireland* (2012). She has published widely on Victorian Ireland in journals such as the *Field Day Review*, *Victorian Literature and Culture*, and *Nineteenth Century Contexts* as well as a number of edited collections. She is currently at work on a book on Irish internationalism in the nineteenth century.

....

RENISA MAWANI (COEDITOR; AUTHOR OF C IS FOR CATTLE AND I IS FOR IBIS) is Professor of Sociology at the University of British Columbia and Chair of the Law and Society Program. She is the author of *Colonial Proximities: Crossracial Encounters and Juridical Truths in British Columbia, 1871–1921* (2009) and *Across*

Oceans of Law: The Komagata Maru and Jurisdiction in the Time of Empire (2018).

....

HEIDI J. NAST (D IS FOR DOG) is Professor of International Studies at DePaul University. Her work centers on theories and ontologies of fertility across different geopolitical economic contexts, drawing heavily on fieldwork, empirical study, and a range of critical social theory and psychoanalysis.

....

MICHAEL A. OSBORNE (Z IS FOR ZEBU) is Professor of History of Science at Oregon State University and Research Professor of Environmental Studies and History at the University of California, Santa Barbara. He also served as president of the Division of History of Science and Technology of the International Union of History and Philosophy of Science and Technology (2017–21). He is the author of *The Emergence of Tropical Medicine in France* (2014) and other studies on the history of medicine, natural history, and popular zoology in France and the French Empire. His current projects include a global history of yellow fever.

....

HARRIET RITVO (Q IS FOR QUAGGA) is the Arthur J. Conner Professor of History at the Massachusetts Insti-

tute of Technology and the author of *The Animal Estate: The English and Other Creatures in the Victorian Age* (1987); *The Platypus and the Mermaid, and Other Figments of the Classifying Imagination* (1997); *The Dawn of Green: Manchester, Thirlmere and Modern Environmentalism* (2009); and *Noble Cows and Hybrid Zebras: Essays on Animals and History* (2010). She is working on a book about wildness and domestication.

....

GEORGE ROBB (F IS FOR FOX) is Professor of History at William Paterson University of New Jersey. He has published widely in the fields of British and American social and cultural history. His most recent book is *Ladies of the Ticker: Women and Wall Street from the Gilded Age to the Great Depression* (2017).

....

JONATHAN SAHA (E IS FOR ELEPHANT) is Associate Professor of Southeast Asian History at the University of Leeds. He specializes in the history of nineteenth- and twentieth-century colonialism in British Burma. His book *Law, Disorder and the Colonial State* (2013), a study of official misconduct in the fin de siècle Burma Delta, explored how the colonial state was experienced and imagined in everyday life. Saha has published on crime, medicine and "madness" in colonial Burma. Over the last few years, he has been working on a history of animals in British Burma, drawing out their intrinsic role in the construction and maintenance of the imperial order.

....

SANDRA SWART (O IS FOR OKAPI) is Professor in the Department of History at Stellenbosch University. She received her DPhil in Modern History from Oxford University in 2001 and simultaneously obtained an MSc (with distinction) in Environmental Change and Management, also at Oxford. She has researched and published widely on the social and environmental history of southern Africa, with a particular focus on the shifting relationship between humans and animals. Swart is an editor of the *South African Historical Journal* and has served on the editorial boards of a number of international journals, including *Environmental History*. She has served as president of the Southern African Historical Society. She has authored and co-authored over sixty peer-reviewed articles and chapters in academic books, coauthored two books, co-edited one book, and is the sole author of *Riding High: Horses, Humans and History in South Africa* (2010).

....

ANGELA THOMPSELL (G IS FOR GIRAFFE) is Associate Professor of History at the College at Brockport, State University of New York. She is interested in the idea of Africa in the West and the everyday encounters that imperialism generated. She has recently completed a comparison of imperialism and international peacekeeping in Africa. Thompsell is currently researching the gendered encounters of African exploration and the life of an imperial travelwriter. She is the author of *Hunting Africa: British Sport, African Knowledge and the Nature of Empire* (2015) and served as the African expert at ThoughtCo from 2014 to 2016.

....

INDEX

Page numbers in italics refer to illustrations.

Derby, Earl of (Edward Smith Stanley), 103, 167, 216

Descent of Man (Darwin), 3, 23

Dewar, Thomas, 210

dholes (wild dogs). *See* dogs

Dickens, Charles, 120

dingoes, 7, 97, 98–100

Dingo Makes Us Human (Rose), 99

disease, 6; cattle and, 40, 223; horses and, 81, 83; mosquitos and, 118–23; vultures and, 191; zebus and, 221–22

dispossession. *See* land appropriation

dogs, 10, 46–52; dingoes contrasted with, 99; and hunting, 33, 64, 65, 67, 97

Dr. Jekyll and Mr. Hyde (Stevenson), 25

Du Chaillu, Paul, 25–26, *206*, 209

Dunlop, R. H. W., 65

East African Mammals (Kingdon), 206

East India Company, 57, 80–83

ecosystems: animal transportation and, 7, 10; boars and, 31, 33; cattle and, 40, 42–43; dogs and, 47; elephants and, 57, 59; foxes and, 64, 67–68; hunting and, 97–98; ibis and, 92; malaria and, 122–23; raccoons and, 159–60; squirrels and, 207–8; vultures and, 190–91; whaling and, 201. *See also* climate change; conservation

Egypt, 9, 73, 89–92, 119, 120–21, 222

elephants, 4, 56–61, 174, 191

Elliot, Henry, 65, 166

endangered species: dingoes, 98; elephants, 60; okapis, 132, 135; squirrels, 210; tigers, 175, 176; vultures, 190–91; whales, 127, 128–29, 201. *See also* extinction

English and Australian Cookery Book (Abbott), 31

English Muscovy Company, 127

evolutionary theory, 4, 23, 25, 89–92, 181–82. *See also* degeneration; natural history; zoology

Ewart, William Cossar, 148–49

extinction, 10–11, 19, 98, 146–49, 176. *See also* endangered species

farming. *See* agriculture

fashion, 8; beaver pelts and, 156; giraffe-inspired, 74; kiwi feathers and, 103, 104, 106–7; raccoon fur and, 156–57; squirrel fur and, 208–9; vulture feathers and, 191; whalebone (baleen) and, 126, 199; yak tails and wool, 214–15

femininity, 8, 27, *164*, 167, 174, 199. *See also* gender; masculinity

folklore: African, 96–98, 207; Australian Aboriginal, 99–100; Egyptian, 89–90; European, 64–65, 181–86, 192–93, 198; Māori, 103; okapis as, 133–34; Polynesian, 32; South Asian, 166

food: boars as, 30–33, 34; cattle as, 10, 39, 40–41, 220, 221, 223, 224; dingoes as, 98; giraffes as, 73, 75; kangaroos as, 32, 42; kiwi as, 104; okapis as, 133; quaggas as, 147; squirrels as, 208; yaks as, 215

Foucault, Michel, 5

Fox, Charles James, 65

foxes, 7, 64–68, 97

France, 9, 51, 74, 88, 90–91, 224

Franklin, Benjamin, 157

Franklin, Jane, 142

Frazer, William, 81

Frobisher, Martin, 181–82

funeral rituals, 190, 221–22

furniture, 58, 76

gambling, 49, 56

Gedeboe people, 192–93, 207

gender, 8–9; in Anglo-Afghan War cartoon, *164*, 167; dogfighting and, 48–49, 52; hunting and, 33–34, 65, 76, 110, 112, 209; raccoons and, 6, 156–58; simian representation and, 25, 27; tigers and, 174–75; unicorns and, 184; whales and, 199. *See also* femininity; masculinity

George IV (king), 73
Ghana, 207
gifts, 32, 47, 73
giraffes, 72–77, 134–35
Gliddon, George, 91
Gordon-Cumming, Constance F.,
   185–86
The Gorilla Hunters (Ballantyne), 25
Great Expectations (Dickens), 120

"Hark! Hark! The Dogs Do Bark!"
   (map), *46*, 51
Hastings, Warren, 214–16
Hawai'i, 32, 39–40
Health Problems of the Empire (Balfour
   and Scott), 191
Hindus, 3, 41–42, 65, 166, 220–21, 223
Hinks, James, 50
History of Quadrupeds (Pennant), 146,
   149, 215
A History of the Birds of New Zealand
   (Buller), *102*, 104
Holmgren, Virginia C., 156
horses, 33, 64, 65, 80–85, 133–34
Hudson, Henry, 127
"human zoos," 74–75
hunting, 8–9; boars, 33–34; conservation and, 147–48; dogs and, 47;
   elephants, 57, 58; foxes, 7, 64, 65–68;
   giraffes, 75–77; jackals, 97–98; kiwi,
   103, 105; lions, 111–14; lynching as
   "coon," 159; okapis, 133; platypuses,
   143; quaggas, 10, 147; raccoons,
   157–58; squirrels, 208–9; tigers, *172*,
   173–75; vultures and, 191, 192; whales,
   10, 126–29, 198–201

ibis, 9, 88–92
*The Ibis: A Quarterly Journal of Orni-
   thology*, *88*, 90
Illustrated Alphabet of Birds, 90
Illustrated Police News, *96*, 99
India: animal brutality in, 3; boar hunting in, 33–34; cattle in 39, 41–42,
   220–21, 223; dogs in, 97; elephants in,
   57, 59–60; foxes in, 65, 66–67; horses

in, 80–85; scorpions in, 166–67; tigers
   in, 172–76; vultures in, 190–91, 193;
   yaks in, 214–15
Indian Rebellion of 1857, 42, 57, 84, *110*,
   111, 174
Indian Ocean, 80–85
Indigenous peoples: Arctic expeditions and, 182; cattle and, 40; dogs
   and, 47; elephants and, 56, 60; giraffes and, 74–75; lions and, 112,
   113–14; mountaineering and, 217;
   ocean management and, 200, 201–2;
   okapis and, 133, 134; platypuses and,
   141–42; in Polynesia, 32–33; raccoons
   and, 155–56; rights of, 104–5, 201–2;
   tiger hunting and, 173–74; whaling
   and, 199. *See also* land appropriation;
   sovereignty
Insectopedia (Raffles), 7–8
insects, 7–8, 118–23, 167
Inuit, 182
Ireland, 26–27, *64*, 65–66, 68, 167

jackals, 7, 67, 96–98, 100
Jamaica, 191
Jones, Charles "Buffalo," 209
John Bull, 17, 18, *154*, 158, *164*, 167
Johnston, Harry, 4, 133–34, 208
Jumbo (elephant), 58–59

kangaroos, 32, 111
Kennel Club, 51
Kenya, 58, 112–13, 191
Keyl, W. F., 47
Kingdon, Jonathan, 206
Kipling, John Lockwood, 3
Kipling, Rudyard, 26
kiwi, 102–7
Knight, Charles, 3, 113
Kreilkamp, Ivan, 7

land appropriation, 6–7; the Anthropocene and, 19; cattle and, 39–40, 104;
   disease control and, 119, 122; kiwi
   conservation and, 104–5; tiger conservation and, 175; whaling and, 128.

transportation: of animals, 6–7, 10; of cattle, 39–43; of dogs, 49; elephants used for, 59–60; of foxes to Australia for hunting, 67; of horses, 80–85; of pigs, 31; of raccoons to Europe and Japan, 159; yaks and, 214–17; of zebus, 17, 222, 223–24; zoos and, 24, 72–73

Transvaal. *See* Cape Colony; South Africa

travel narratives: apes in, 24, 25–26; as bestiaries, 4; narwhals in, 185–86; squirrels in, 209–10; yaks in, 214, 215–16. *See also* adventure stories

Trinidad, 92, 191

Tryon, Thomas, 223

Turner, Samuel, *214*, 215–16

Types of Mankind (Nott and Gliddon), 91

Uganda, 4

Uganda Protectorate (Johnston), 4

Unbeaten Tracks in Japan (Bird), 185

unicorns, 12, 133–34, 180–86

United States: conservation in, 147, 201; dogs in, 49; fear of slave rebellion, 26; fox symbolism in, 65; ibis, race, and evolutionary theory in, 91; and imperial authority, 111; and raccoons, 6, 17, 154–59; and tropical medicine, 119–22; and whaling, 9, 128, 200; *Xerus* symbolism in, 210; zebus in, 223–25

van der Merwe, N. J., 98

Van Diemen's Land. *See* Australia

vegetarianism, 223

Victoria (queen), 24, 47, 167

vultures, 190–94

Wahunsenecawh, 155

warfare: elephants and, 57, 59; horses and, 80–85; scorpions and, 166; vultures and, 193–94; yaks and, 217

Waterman, Jane, 207

Wells, Carolyn, 210

West, John, 32

Whitman, Walt, 3

whales, 9, 10, 126–29, 198–202

Wildlife under the Equator, Narrated for Young People (Du Chaillu), *206*, 209

Xerus, 206–11

The Yak of Tartary (Stubbs), *214*, 215–16

yaks, 214–18

Yolen, Jane, 224

zebras, 148–50

zebus, 10, 17, 220–25. *See also* cattle

zoology: apes and, 22–24; as bestiary, 3–4; cryptozoology, 136; jackals and, 98; kiwi and, 103–4; and nationalism, 73, 76; okapis and, 134–35; quaggas and, 148–50; scorpions and, 168; squirrels and, 206–7

Zoological Society of London. *See* London Zoo (London Zoological Gardens)

zoos and menageries: apes in, 24; elephants in, 57–59; giraffes in, 72–75, 76; "human," 74–75; lions in, 113–14; okapis in, 134; platypuses in, 143; quaggas in, 147; yaks in, 215, 216; zebus in, 222, 223–24

Zulu people, 192